POLITICAL PARTIES

Published in association with the Centre for Canadian Studies at Mount Allison University. Information on the Canadian Democratic Audit project can be found at www.CanadianDemocraticAudit.ca.

Advisory Group

William Cross, Director (Mount Allison University)
R. Kenneth Carty (University of British Columbia)
Elisabeth Gidengil (McGill University)
Richard Sigurdson (University of New Brunswick)
Frank Strain (Mount Allison University)
Michael Tucker (Mount Allison University)

Titles

John Courtney, *Elections*
William Cross, *Political Parties*
Elisabeth Gidengil, André Blais, Neil Nevitte, and Richard Nadeau, *Citizens*
David Docherty, *Legislatures*
Jennifer Smith, *Federalism*
Lisa Young and Joanna Everitt, *Advocacy Groups*
Darin Barney, *Communications Technology*
Ian Greene, *The Courts*
Graham White, *Cabinets and First Ministers*

POLITICAL PARTIES

William Cross

UBCPress

15 14 13 12 11 10 09 08 07 06   5 4 3

Printed in Canada on acid-free paper that is 100% post-consumer recycled, processed chlorine-free, and printed with vegetable-based, low-VOC inks.

Library and Archives Canada Cataloguing in Publication

Cross, William P. (William Paul), 1962-
  Political parties / William Cross.

  (The Canadian democratic audit ; 2)
  Includes bibliographical references and index.
  ISBN 978-0-7748-1101-9 (set). –
  ISBN 978-0-7748-0940-5 (bound); ISBN 978-0-7748-0941-2 (pbk)

  1. Political parties – Canada. 2. Canada – Politics and government.
I. Title. II. Series: Canadian democratic audit ; 2.

JL195.C76 2004   324.271   C2004-901745-4

Canadä

UBC Press gratefully acknowledges the financial support for our publishing program of the Government of Canada through the Book Publishing Industry Development Program (BPIDP), and of the Canada Council for the Arts, and the British Columbia Arts Council.

The Centre for Canadian Studies thanks the Harold Crabtree Foundation for its support of the Canadian Democratic Audit project.

This book has been published with the help of the K.D. Srivastava Fund.

Copy editor: Sarah Wight
Text design: Peter Ross, Counterpunch
Typesetter: Artegraphica Design Co. Ltd.
Proofreader: Gail Copeland

UBC Press
The University of British Columbia
2029 West Mall
Vancouver, BC V6T 1Z2
604-822-5959 / Fax: 604-822-6083
www.ubcpress.ca

Contents

FIGURES AND TABLES

Figures

Tables

Foreword

This volume is part of the Canadian Democratic Audit series. The objective of this series is to consider how well Canadian democracy is performing at the outset of the twenty-first century. In recent years, political and opinion leaders, government commissions, academics, citizen groups, and the popular press have all identified a "democratic deficit" and "democratic malaise" in Canada. These characterizations often are portrayed as the result of a substantial decline in Canadians' confidence in their democratic practices and institutions. Indeed, Canadians are voting in record low numbers, many are turning away from the traditional political institutions, and a large number are expressing declining confidence in both their elected politicians and the electoral process.

Nonetheless, Canadian democracy continues to be the envy of much of the rest of the world. Living in a relatively wealthy and peaceful society, Canadians hold regular elections in which millions cast ballots. These elections are largely fair, efficient, and orderly events. They routinely result in the selection of a government with no question about its legitimate right to govern. Developing democracies from around the globe continue to look to Canadian experts for guidance in establishing electoral practices and democratic institutions. Without a doubt, Canada is widely seen as a leading example of successful democratic practice.

Given these apparently competing views, the time is right for a comprehensive examination of the state of Canadian democracy. Our purposes are to conduct a systematic review of the operations of Canadian democracy, to listen to what others have to say about Canadian democracy, to assess its strengths and weaknesses, to consider where there are opportunities for advancement, and to evaluate popular reform proposals.

A democratic audit requires the setting of benchmarks for evaluation of the practices and institutions to be considered. This necessarily involves substantial consideration of the meaning of democracy.

"Democracy" is a contested term and we are not interested here in striking a definitive definition. Nor are we interested in a theoretical model applicable to all parts of the world. Rather we are interested in identifying democratic benchmarks relevant to Canada in the twenty-first century. In selecting these we were guided by the issues raised in the current literature on Canadian democratic practice and by the concerns commonly raised by opinion leaders and found in public opinion data. We have settled on three benchmarks: public participation, inclusiveness, and responsiveness. We believe that any contemporary definition of Canadian democracy must include institutions and decision-making practices that are defined by public participation, that this participation include all Canadians, and that government outcomes respond to the views of Canadians.

While settling on these guiding principles, we have not imposed a strict set of democratic criteria on all of the evaluations that together constitute the Audit. Rather, our approach allows the auditors wide latitude in their evaluations. While all auditors keep the benchmarks of participation, inclusiveness, and responsiveness central to their examinations, each adds additional criteria of particular importance to the subject he or she is considering. We believe this approach of identifying unifying themes, while allowing for divergent perspectives, enhances the project by capturing the robustness of the debate surrounding democratic norms and practices.

We decided at the outset to cover substantial ground and to do so in a relatively short period. These two considerations, coupled with a desire to respond to the most commonly raised criticisms of the contemporary practice of Canadian democracy, result in a series that focuses on public institutions, electoral practices, and new phenomena that are likely to affect democratic life significantly. The series includes volumes that examine key public decision-making bodies: legislatures, the courts, and cabinets and government. The structures of our democratic system are considered in volumes devoted to questions of federalism and the electoral system. The ways in which citizens participate in electoral politics and policy making are a crucial component of the project, and thus we include studies of interest groups and political parties. The desire and capacity of Canadians for meaningful participation in public life is also the subject of a volume. Finally, the challenges and opportunities raised by new communication technologies is also considered. The Audit does not include studies devoted to the status of particular groups of Canadians. Rather than separate out Aboriginals, women, new Canadians, and others, these groups are treated together with all Canadians throughout the Audit.

In all, this series includes nine volumes examining specific areas of Canadian democratic life. A tenth, synthetic volume provides an overall assessment and makes sense out of the different approaches and findings found in the rest of the series. Our examination is not exhaustive. Canadian democracy is a vibrant force, the status of which can never be fully captured at one time. Nonetheless the areas we consider involve many of the pressing issues currently facing democracy in Canada. We do not expect to have the final word on this subject. Rather, we hope to encourage others to pursue similar avenues of inquiry.

A project of this scope cannot be accomplished without the support of many individuals. At the top of the list of those deserving credit are the members of the Canadian Democratic Audit team. From the very beginning, the Audit has been a team effort. This outstanding group of academics has spent many hours together, defining the scope of the project, prodding each other on questions of Canadian democracy, and most importantly, supporting one another throughout the endeavour, all with good humour. To Darin Barney, André Blais, Kenneth Carty, John Courtney, David Docherty, Joanna Everitt, Elisabeth Gidengil, Ian Greene, Richard Nadeau, Neil Nevitte, Richard Sigurdson, Jennifer Smith, Frank Strain, Michael Tucker, Graham White, and Lisa Young I am forever grateful.

The Centre for Canadian Studies at Mount Allison University has been my intellectual home for several years. The Centre, along with the Harold Crabtree Foundation, has provided the necessary funding and other assistance necessary to see this project through to fruition. At Mount Allison University, Peter Ennals provided important support to this project when others were skeptical; Wayne MacKay and Michael Fox have continued this support since their respective arrivals on campus; and Joanne Goodrich and Peter Loewen have provided important technical and administrative help.

The University of British Columbia Press, particularly its senior acquisitions editor, Emily Andrew, has been a partner in this project from the very beginning. Emily has been involved in every important decision and has done much to improve the result. Camilla Jenkins has overseen the copyediting and production process and in doing so has made these books better. Scores of Canadian and international political scientists have participated in the project as commentators at our public conferences, as critics at our private meetings, as providers of quiet advice, and as referees of the volumes. The list is too long to name them all, but David Cameron, Sid Noel, Leslie Seidle, Jim Bickerton, Alexandra Dobrowolsky, Livianna Tossutti, Janice Gross Stein, and Frances Abele all deserve special recognition for their contributions. We are also grateful to the Canadian Study of Parliament Group, which partnered with us for our inaugural conference in Ottawa in November 2001.

Emma and Vera have allowed me the time and space necessary to complete this project. Their patience and support are much appreciated.

Finally, this series is dedicated to all of the men and women who contribute to the practice of Canadian democracy. Whether as active participants in parties, groups, courts, or legislatures, or in the media and the universities, without them Canadian democracy would not survive.

William Cross
Director, The Canadian Democratic Audit
Sackville, New Brunswick

Political Parties

AUDITING CANADA'S POLITICAL PARTIES 1

Political parties are the central players in Canadian democracy. Many of us experience politics only through parties. They connect us to our democratic institutions. We vote in elections in which parties choose the local and prime ministerial candidates and dominate campaign discourse. Our legislatures are structured along party lines. Policy debates are shaped by the parties represented in the legislatures, and they determine which interests are heard. Parties are so central to our democratic life that if they are not participatory our politics cannot be participatory, if they are not inclusive our politics cannot be inclusive, and if they are not responsive then our politics cannot be responsive. Parties lie at the heart of Canadian democracy, and an examination of the state of our parties is an essential component of the Canadian Democratic Audit.

Whatever the relative merits of representative and direct democracy, a modern state with the geographic scope and population of Canada has no realistic alternative to the representative form. In Canada, these representatives are party men and women, who are the link between voters and policy outcomes. As William Chandler and Alan Siaroff (1991, 192) have written, "Parties operate as the crucial intermediaries linking rulers and ruled. The most basic party function is that of representation involving the translation of public opinion to political leaders." Given this need for representation, parties are an integral part of contemporary democratic practice. Students of comparative modern democracies have long concluded that the democratic form is "unthinkable" without parties and that "parties are inevitable" (Dalton and Wattenberg 2000).

In recent decades, however, Canadians have become increasingly dissatisfied with the role parties are playing as intermediaries between grassroots voters and elite decision makers. The Royal Commission on Electoral Reform and Party Financing (1991, 1:208) found that "more and more Canadians, including party members, are critical of the way parties select their candidates and leaders, the control party officials appear to exercise over their supporters in Parliament, the behaviour of the parties during elections, their failure to change party organization and membership to reflect Canadian society, and their shortcomings in providing significant opportunities for political participation."

Canadians are not alone in these sentiments. Dalton and Wattenberg (2000), two keen observers of modern democracies, have concluded that there is widespread dissatisfaction with the role played by political parties in many contemporary industrial democracies. Nonetheless, although Canadians are increasingly skeptical of the ways in which their parties operate, they continue to see them as an essential part of their democratic life. Indicative of this are public opinion polling data suggesting that while a majority of voters are dissatisfied with the performance of their political institutions (including parties) and believe their politicians to be unresponsive and out of touch, three-quarters of Canadians maintain the belief that "without parties, there can't be true democracy" (Blais and Gidengil 1991, 20). Considering the crucial role parties play in linking voters to the practice of democracy, the health of parties is a crucial component in the welfare of every contemporary democratic state. If voter confidence in democratic life is to be enhanced, parties must be a key part of any revitalization.

In recent decades, political parties have been the area of Canadian democratic life to sustain the most significant transformation. The cast and character of Canada's federal parties and party competition changed dramatically at the end of the twentieth century. The general election of 1993 ushered in a new party system marked by, among other things, an increase in the number of parties, the rise of regional parties, significant fragmentation of both voter support and political communication, and a change in the norms of party democracy. This was the third time in our history that Canadians had rid themselves of a long-established pattern of party competition and party organization in favour of something new (Carty, Cross, and Young 2000).

Although other sorts of institutional change have been advocated and supported by public opinion, there has been little additional reform. For example, while voters expressed substantial dissatisfaction with the functioning of Parliament, focusing on the concentration of power in the prime minister's office and the lack of a meaningful role for MPs, things have only gotten worse in this regard (as witnessed in two books, Jeffrey Simpson's *The friendly dictatorship* [2001] and Donald Savoie's *Governing from the centre: The concentration of power in Canadian politics* [1999]). Similarly, widespread support for the use of direct democracy has not resulted in significant change. A few provinces have dabbled with referendum and recall legislation, but for the most part these have been failed efforts that do not represent a fundamental shift in the country's political behaviour. Much criticism has been levelled at the unelected and nonrepresentative Senate; nonetheless, Senate reform appears as far away today as ever. There has also been much criticism of our electoral system, with increasing public calls for some form of proportional representation, but our electoral system also remains unchanged. What clearly did change in the wake of voter antipathy at the end of the last century was the Canadian party system. And given the privileged place of parties in both electoral campaigns and law making, surely Canadians are right in directing their efforts at the party system.

Canada's political institutions, and much of the country itself, were built by political parties, and there is no doubt that at the outset of the twenty-first century parties remain the linchpins of Canadian democracy. Crucial aspects of our politics, such as candidate recruitment, leadership selection, election campaigning, public policy agenda setting, and governing, are projects dominated by the parties. Given their importance and the dramatic changes to the party system in recent years, an investigation into the democratic status of Canada's political parties is timely.

The Audit Approach

The Canadian Democratic Audit project centres on the benchmarks of participation, inclusiveness, and responsiveness. Rather than discussing theoretically the democratic possibilities and nuances of party activity, my task is to measure their performance in terms of these benchmarks. In applying them to political parties, I have taken a functional approach. Consistent with the Audit's framework, this involves identifying the principal responsibilities of Canada's parties and then considering how participatory, inclusive, and responsive they are in carrying them out. As a result, this book is not about the Canadian party system as such, but rather a consideration of the internal workings of the parties, examining them as democratic organizations. Readers interested in a contemporary exploration of the party system should see *Rebuilding Canadian party politics* (Carty, Cross, and Young 2000). The discussion in this volume focuses primarily on party life outside of the legislatures. In separate volumes in this series, David Docherty (2004) examines the state of Canada's legislatures, and Graham White (forthcoming 2005) considers questions relating to cabinet and governance.

The benchmark terms "participation," "inclusiveness," and "responsiveness" are straightforward and are used in their ordinary senses. Accordingly, their meaning should be readily apparent. In measuring participation, primary consideration is given to the numbers of Canadians involved in the various party activities, as well as to the reasons why more Canadians are not participating. Widespread grassroots participation in public decision making is a hallmark of democratic practice, and both the participatory opportunities offered by the parties and the obstacles they impose to participation are central to this investigation. Similarly, the discussion relating to inclusiveness assesses how representative those participating in parties are of the general population. Special emphasis is placed on the efforts parties make to increase (and the barriers they impose on) participatory opportunities for those groups who have been traditionally under-represented in Canadian public life. Consideration of responsiveness focuses on the quality of participatory opportunities and the connec-tion between citizens' participation and outcomes. Even fully inclu-sive participation is relatively meaningless if it has no identifiable effect on outcomes. Canada's brokerage parties have long been criticized as elite driven and nonresponsive to their local partisans. Throughout this examination, differences between the older brokerage parties and their newer, more ideological competitors are highlighted.

The four principal activities of parties identified and examined here are policy development, candidate recruitment and selection, leadership selection, and election campaigning. These are among the central democratic functions and are consistent with the roles assigned to parties in most Western democracies (see, for example, King 1969). Consideration is also given to the norms of party member-ship. Canada's parties are membership organizations, and participa-tion in most of their activities is limited to their members. A separate chapter examines questions relating to the financing of party activity.

The analysis focuses on the five principal federal parties (the Bloc Québécois, Canadian Alliance, Liberals, New Democrats, and Progres-sive Conservatives). The Liberal and Conservative parties date back to the nineteenth century. They are both "big tent," ideologically flexible parties and the only ones to have governed at the federal level. The New Democratic Party emerged in the 1960s as an ideologically left-of-centre alternative. Occasionally successful at winning power at the provincial level, the NDP has never won more than one-fifth of the national vote. The Reform and Bloc Québécois arose largely out of the constitutional struggles of the late 1980s and early 1990s. They both achieved some immediate success and, with essentially regional bases of support, have finished second and third in recent elections. In 2000 the Reform Party became the Canadian Alliance; references here to

Reform and the Alliance are to different periods of the same party (for a full discussion of the evolution of the Canadian party system, see Carty, Cross, and Young 2000).

In the fall of 2003, the Canadian Alliance and Progressive Conservative parties began a process aimed at transforming themselves into a single Conservative Party of Canada. Although the process was successful, it is far too premature to consider the impact on the Canadian party system in this book. The best available evidence of what the new entity will prove itself to be is the complexion of its two constituent parties. Accordingly, the experiences of both the Alliance and the Progressive Conservative parties are included in this analysis. A few words about the new party are included in the postscript.

Substantial consideration is also given to provincial party developments. As discussed in Chapter 2, the deeply federal nature of Canadian society is reflected in the parties' organizational structures and results in distinct federal and provincial party systems. Provincial parties have led the way in adopting new methods of leadership selection and in experimenting with different types of campaign finance reform. These provincial experiences are drawn upon in the relevant chapters.

Several standards are used to assess the parties' performances in fulfilling their identified functions. The first is change over time, with the focus on whether parties are becoming increasingly participatory, inclusive, and responsive. The second standard is whether the parties are meeting contemporary democratic expectations. While this is not always easy to measure, these assessments are based on survey data, behavioural patterns, and political observation. And, while the Audit is not a comparative project, experiences in other Western democracies are occasionally useful in considering whether the patterns observed are uniquely Canadian and whether reform alternatives might enhance party democracy. This is necessarily a somewhat subjective exercise and different "auditors" might well reach different conclusions.

The benchmarks framing the Audit project suggest that citizen participation in public decision making is always good, and that the more the better. Of course, democracy is a more nuanced proposition. A respected body of literature in Canadian political science argues for constraints on public participation, suggesting that the cleavages that divide Canadians (language, geography, religion) are best overcome through public decision-making methods characterized by elite accommodation (for early renditions of this argument, see Siegfried [1904] 1966; Dawson 1947). The argument is that representative elites, committed to the maintenance of the federation, are better able to engage in the necessary compromises than are citizens at large. While this rationale is generally considered valid, the practice of elite accommodation has been largely disavowed by public opinion in recent years (Clarke et al. 1996). Nonetheless, the concept offers an important reminder of the brokerage and accommodative roles traditionally played by Canada's national parties and accordingly is considered throughout this analysis. The brokerage parties have been challenged for voter loyalty in recent elections by more ideological parties and interest groups. The dynamics of this tension are also explored.

While it would be easy to point to all that works well with Canada's parties and to pat ourselves on the back for this, such an exercise would be of little use. More important than self-praise is identification of the areas where party democracy is falling short, particularly those areas where voters' democratic expectations are outpacing the performance of the parties. We know that at the outset of the new century, Canadians' satisfaction with their political system is qualified at best. As illustrated in Figure 1.1, voter turnout has declined dramatically in the past twenty years. Similarly, voters' confidence in their political institutions and representatives has dropped sharply. When Canadians were asked to score political parties on a scale of 1 to 100, the mean ranking declined by almost 50 percent between 1968 and 2000 (Carty, Cross, and Young 2000, 29).

As mentioned at the outset, these phenomena are not uniquely Canadian. Voter turnout is declining in many nations, and there is convincing evidence of widespread democratic dissatisfaction (see Pharr and Putnam 2000). The challenge facing those interested in restoring voter confidence is to identify reform alternatives that may begin to reconnect voters to their political institutions. While this

Figure 1.1

Voter turnout in recent federal elections

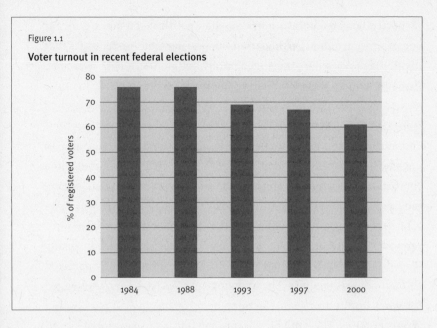

task goes well beyond a consideration of political parties, the central place of parties in our democratic life makes them a key component of any reform initiatives. This book is therefore an attempt to contribute to this discussion as it relates to our political parties.

The Plan of the Book

This book is the culmination of more than a decade of close observation of Canada's political parties. The primary data used in the analysis were gathered in a number of ways. Formal interviews were conducted with several dozen federal and provincial party officials, staff members, and political operatives such as advertisers, pollsters, tour directors, and media consultants. As well, many party activists were engaged in less formal conversations at provincial and federal leadership conventions, party headquarters, candidate training sessions, candidate nomination contests, policy conventions, campaign kickoffs, and campaign storefronts. Data were also gathered through several large mail surveys: in separate surveys, federal riding association presidents and thousands of provincial and federal party members provided information relating to their party experiences and their views regarding party democracy. The federal parties also provided access to their materials deposited with the National Archives. Together, these various sources provide a rich picture of political party life in Canada.

In considering party democracy, one must first tackle the question of what is the party. When we discuss the Liberal Party of Canada, we may be referring to Liberal members of the House of Commons, to card-carrying members of the extraparliamentary party, or to those voters who consider themselves to be Liberal supporters. This question emerges throughout this book. For example, in the area of policy making there is always tension between the parliamentary parties and the grassroots membership regarding who should determine a party's policy positions. Similarly, parties restrict participation in leadership selection and candidate nomination to their members, with the result that most of their electoral supporters are not eligible to participate. Even the concept of extraparliamentary membership means different things at different times. When we speak of party members participating in policy making, we are talking about a relatively small group of partisans who belong to the parties between elections. By contrast, membership during candidate nomination and leadership contests is far more expansive – often several times larger than the interelection membership. In the chapters that follow, consideration is given to the questions of what the appropriate party decision-making body is in each area, and what the parties' current approaches to membership mean in terms of party democracy.

This book begins with an examination of party membership. Making use of data collected through a large survey of federal party members, Chapter 2 considers how accessible party membership is, how many Canadians belong, which Canadians belong, what motivates voters to join parties, how active members are, what activities they engage in, and how satisfied they are with the participatory opportunities afforded them. This chapter concludes that a significant portion of members is dissatisfied with party decision making, principally because the parties have built little capacity to involve local activists in policy study and development on a sustained basis. As discussed in Chapter 3, this is one of the great failings of our parties. Parties, outside of Parliament, play only a sporadic and often superficial role in preparing policy alternatives for their parliamentary wings. Instead, Canadian parties have concentrated on elite recruitment and electoral activity.

Parties exercise a near-total monopoly over the recruitment and selection of candidates for the provincial and federal legislatures. While scores of independent candidates appear on the ballot in each election, the winning candidates are almost always party nominees. Chapter 4 considers how well the parties are doing in nominating candidates who are representative of Canadian society and the role local activists play in these decisions. Leadership selection is also a central activity of the extraparliamentary parties. Chapter 5 examines the evolution of leadership selection processes and evaluates the different methods being used in terms of the Audit's benchmarks. Special attention is paid to the debate between supporters of selection by elite conventions and those favouring votes by the entire membership.

The parties' electoral campaign efforts are assessed in Chapter 6. In addition to selecting both local and prime ministerial candidates, parties dominate political activity and discourse during election campaigns. The chapter considers the role afforded local partisans in party campaigning and the recent movements toward greater professionalization and centralization of campaign activity. While it is impossible to imagine federal or provincial election campaigns without political parties, not all party activity during elections is to be commended. For the most part, parties are failing to connect the efforts of their grassroots volunteers with their central campaign activities.

Democratic elections are expensive endeavours. Since the early 1970s Canada has had a comprehensive regulatory scheme governing the raising and spending of money by political parties and their candidates. Regulating party and election financing is essential to maintaining public confidence in democratic life. Significant changes to this regulatory system were adopted in 2003, and the likely effects of these reforms are examined in Chapter 7.

The final chapter unites the findings of this investigation and suggests four sets of reform proposals aimed at increasing participation, inclusiveness, and responsiveness in our political parties. These are strengthening the parties' capacity for policy study and development through establishment of party policy foundations, opening up the candidate nomination and leadership selection processes to include participation by nonmembers, adoption of some form of proportional representation to encourage parties and their activists to participate in campaign activity in all parts of the country, and further reforms to Canada's campaign finance legislation aimed at increasing parties' responsiveness to voters and making candidacy for elected office more accessible.

Not everyone will agree with the conclusions reached here, but I hope they will encourage others to advance their own reform proposals and encourage our parties to take seriously the need to build stronger bridges between Canadians and their democratic institutions.

2

POLITICAL PARTIES
AS MEMBERSHIP ORGANIZATIONS
WITH LISA YOUNG

One of the core responsibilities assigned to parties is to serve as a bridge between civil society and government. In complex societies like Canada, parties are responsible for aggregating citizen interests and articulating them in the political sphere. The fulfillment of this responsibility requires that the parties as a group provide meaningful opportunities for all citizens to participate. In some ways the Canadian parties are well situated for this task. Through their local constituency branches, they exist in communities across the country. Citizens wishing to participate in public life need not travel to the seat of government in Ottawa, nor mount an issue or political campaign on their own. Instead, they can join with other like-minded individuals in their local community and participate in political life through the party of their choice. In doing so, they join together with Canadians from other regions and, through the strength of their numbers, collectively exercise influence in party and public decision making.

This is the promise of Canada's political parties. In this chapter this ideal is put to the test with an examination of the following questions: How many Canadians belong to political parties? How inclusive are the parties' memberships? What motivates party members? What do members do? Are they satisfied with the participatory opportunities afforded them? An examination of membership provides a portrait of how participatory parties are, how inclusive they are of different segments of Canadian society, and how responsive they are to the views of their activists. Only through membership do ordinary Canadians have access to party decision making. The parties' grassroots members play an influential role in leadership selection and candidate nomination, and they are engaged in an ongoing struggle with the parliamentary parties for influence in policy making. By contrast, no party decision making is open to nonmembers.

Canada's political parties have two categories of members. The first are committed activists who maintain their membership year after year; the second group are attracted to a leadership or nomination contest, join the party for the sole purpose of participating in this one event, and then let their membership lapse. Party membership routinely increases by 200 to 300 percent during periods of candidate nomination and leadership selection contests. Even in the NDP, a party with a weaker tradition of membership mobilization than the others, the number of members increased by almost 50 percent in the run-up to its 2003 leadership contest. This chapter, and Chapter 3 on policy study and development, focus on activist members. Nomination and leadership contests, and the membership recruitment drives that are often an integral part of them, are examined in Chapters 4 and 5.

The data used in this chapter were gathered by means of a mailback survey of approximately 11,000 members of the five federal parties in the spring of 2000. Those surveyed were party members who joined or renewed their membership in an interelection period when no nomination or leadership contests were under way. Close to 4,000 responses were received for a response rate of 36 percent.

Party Membership and the Canadian Party System

Two aspects of the current Canadian party system need to be considered when examining the status of party membership: federalism, and the changes that took place during the 1990s. First, the party system reflects the fact that Canada is a highly decentralized federation. This means there are different parties and party systems both federally and provincially. Some voters belong to the same party at both levels, others to a party at one level and not the other, and still others belong to different parties at the provincial and federal levels.

This trend toward separation of the federal and provincial party systems has recently sharpened. Of the five major federal parties, only three compete for office at the provincial level. Both the Canadian Alliance and the Bloc Québécois contest only federal elections. Similarly, a number of major provincial parties do not exist at the federal level, such as the Parti Québécois and Saskatchewan Party.

Even when a party label exists at both the provincial and federal levels, it may represent different places on the ideological spectrum. The Liberal Party in British Columbia is an example of this. The federal party is viewed by voters in the province as slightly left of centre. It has not fared well recently as the Canadian Alliance won a large majority of the province's seats in the 1993, 1997, and 2000 elections. At the provincial level (with no Alliance or Conservative parties competing), the Liberals compete as a right-of-centre alternative to the New Democrats, whom they removed from office in the 2001 provincial election. Many provincial Liberals do not support the party at the federal level and vice versa. Similarly, in Alberta and Ontario, the Conservatives have elected large majority governments in recent provincial campaigns while the federal party has been virtually shut out.

In recognition of this federal/provincial dichotomy, parties with the same name often operate completely independent of one another at the different levels. For example, in the Progressive Conservative Party the provincial and federal parties have been organizationally independent of one another in every province. It is unclear what relationship the newly merged federal Alliance/Progressive Conservative party will have with provincial Progressive Conservative parties, many of which, particularly in Atlantic Canada, may not wish to be associated with the old Canadian Alliance Party. Federal and provincial Liberal parties operate separately in the four largest provinces (Ontario,

Quebec, British Columbia, and Alberta) and jointly in the six smaller provinces. Where the parties operate separate wings they have independent federal and provincial organizations with separate staffs and offices, and of course different party members.

Only the New Democratic Party is organized in an integrated fashion. Except in the province of Quebec, it operates as a true federation. The other nine provincial parties, along with their territorial counterparts, together comprise the federal party. Members join the party only at the provincial level and by doing so automatically become a federal party member. When joining a provincial section, members are required to affirm that they do not hold membership in another federal or provincial party.

The federal nature of party membership has important implications in terms of the Audit's benchmarks. Lack of coherency between the federal and provincial levels means that interested Canadians have to join and participate in two parties – one at each level. An environmental activist who succeeds in having a pro-environment policy adopted by her provincial Liberal Party must wage a separate effort to have the federal party also adopt her preferred position (and vice versa). In terms of participation, the existence of two levels provides more and varied points of access, but requires greater commitment because of their bifurcation. In terms of responsiveness, the separation between federal and provincial parties allows distinct provincial parties to emerge across the country, reflecting the views of local members and not hemmed in by the concerns of the national party. The fact that provincial parties of the same name are not bound by the positions adopted by their federal cousins explains the dramatic differences in approaches taken by Conservative parties in different provinces, reflecting their local traditions and political cultures. Alberta and Ontario Conservatives in the past decade have adopted a neoconservative approach to governing, while Conservative governments in the Atlantic provinces have been considerably more centrist.

The second important consideration is the fundamental change the Canadian party system underwent in the last decade. Prior to 1990, federal electoral politics was dominated by the Liberal and Conservative parties. Both of these were elite-driven parties without national membership programs. Membership in the parties was meaningful only as a requisite for participation in candidate nomination and leadership selection processes. The NDP, perennially finishing third place at the federal level during this period, was the exception in being much more grassroots driven. It often attempted to make electoral hay out of this difference from the two larger parties.

The election of 1993 ushered in an important shift in this balance with the success of the Reform Party and the Bloc Québécois. Both of the new parties were committed to more inclusive norms of party democracy than were the Liberals and Conservatives. One of the founding principles of Reform was that it was to be a grassroots-driven party. The party consciously set itself apart from its opponents by attempting to develop a direct link with its members and by providing them with a meaningful role in party decision making. Several of the key decisions made early on by the party (whether to contest elections in central and eastern Canada and whether to pursue the United Alternative project) were decided by a referendum of the party's members. Reform was the first federal party to permit voters to join directly through the national office, and the Bloc soon followed suit.

The Conservatives, largely in response to Reform's electoral success, included a national membership program in a package of "democratizing" reforms adopted in 1995. The federal Liberal Party still has essentially no members. Provincial parties have members, as do the provincial wings of the federal party. Members can only join through these entities and not through the party headquarters in Ottawa. Nonetheless, the party has moved modestly, though less so than the others, to increase the influence of its grassroots activists in party decision making. All of the parties prefer to present themselves as grassroots driven, which according to most public opinion polling is consistent with voter preferences (for more on this see Young and Cross 2002b). These developments make an investigation into the norms of party membership timely.

Who Belongs?

Canada's political parties are not successful at attracting large numbers of committed members. A recent survey of Canadians found that 16 percent claim to have belonged to a political party at some point in their life (Howe and Northrup 2002). This number is probably somewhat exaggerated by those political partisans who have never formally joined a party, but nonetheless consider themselves members. In the past decade, at any given point between elections, between 1 and 2 percent of Canadians are estimated to have belonged to a federal political party. This compares unfavourably with other Western democracies. For example, voters in the United Kingdom are three times as likely as Canadians to belong to a political party, Danish voters seven times as likely, and Finnish voters thirteen times as likely (Carty 1991). Only in Australia is the participation rate as low as in Canada. Nonetheless, while a higher percentage of voters belong to parties in most other countries, evidence from a number of them suggests that, as in Canada, their membership numbers have been declining over the past few decades (Scarrow 2000).

The question of why more Canadians do not belong to a party is difficult to answer. Membership requirements are not particularly onerous. Generally the qualifications for party membership are few, as the parties try, at least in a formal sense, to be as open and inclusive as possible. Indeed, membership in parties is less restrictive than is voting eligibility in general elections. Noncitizens and those not yet of voting age (eighteen) are permitted to join. The only formal requirement is usually the payment of a small fee (often ten dollars) and completion of a short membership form. Occasionally a party may also require applicants to affirm that they do not currently belong to another party, though this is the exception and not the rule.

As discussed later in this chapter, the likely reason for the low membership rate is that Canadians do not see any great benefit to be gained through party membership. As recounted in Chapter 1, a growing number of Canadians have lost confidence in parties. This sentiment is reflected in a recent survey finding that by a three-to-one margin Canadians think joining an interest group is a more effective way of working for political change than joining a party (Howe and Northrup 2002). As we will see, even those who belong to the parties are not particularly satisfied with the participatory opportunities they offer. Consistent with this, there is evidence that Canadians view parties as too hierarchical and are increasingly less interested in belonging to elite-driven institutions (for a general discussion of this value change, see Nevitte 1996).

Those who do belong to political parties are not representative of Canadian society at large. As illustrated in Table 2.1, party members tend to be well educated, male, old, and born in Canada. Almost two-thirds of all members are men; only in the Liberal and New Democratic parties are women represented in roughly equal numbers. Both of these parties, unlike the Conservatives or Alliance, contain separate women's groups and have rules regarding gender representation at party conventions. While some criticize these practices for ghettoizing female members, the affirmative approach these parties take toward attracting women likely helps to explain their greater proportion of female members. This difference between the parties is not wholly explainable on the basis of women's party preference. While the Alliance receives significantly more votes from men than from women, the same is not true for the Conservatives.

Women are underrepresented not only in the parties' memberships but also in decision-making positions at the local level. Several

Table 2.1

Sociodemographic characteristics of party members

	Bloc Québécois (%)	Canadian Alliance (%)	Liberals (%)	New Democrats (%)	Progressive Conservatives (%)
Male	64	68	53	54	67
Under 40	13	6	19	9	12
Over 65	37	59	33	40	53
Attended university	53	41	65	57	63
Born in Canada	97	86	86	80	88
Francophone	100	1	28	4	6

Political Parties As Membership Organizations

studies have found women to be underrepresented in positions such as constituency association presidents. The trend seems to be that the more influential the position is in party decision making, the less likely a woman is to occupy it. (For more on this, see Bashevkin 1993 and Young 2000.)

The average age of party members is fifty-nine, and almost half are sixty-five or older. The parties on the right, the Alliance and Conservatives, have a significantly older membership than do the other parties. Only the Liberals have significant representation among younger Canadians. Slightly more than one in ten Liberal members are under thirty, compared with one in twenty members of the other parties.

Party members are significantly better educated than voters at large, with six in ten having attended university. Alliance members differ in this regard as only four in ten of them have attended university. However, given that the overall university participation rate in Canada is about 23 percent, non-university attendees are significantly underrepresented in all of the parties.

Nine in ten party members were born in Canada, with almost all being of European ancestry. This contrasts with approximately 18 percent of the general population being born abroad. Less than 5 percent of members report an ancestry other than European, including a handful of members of Aboriginal, Asian, Middle Eastern, and African descent. And 99 percent of party members are Canadian citizens.

Even those party members recruited to the parties within the past few years are relatively old and overwhelmingly of European descent. The average age of members who joined after the 1993 election is fifty-three, and only one in ten of these new members is under twenty-five. Thus it is not the case that members are old simply because they have belonged to the party for a long time; rather, the attraction of party membership lies disproportionately (and increasingly) with older voters. And even though patterns of immigration have changed dramatically in recent years, resulting in a significant increase in the number of non-European immigrants, these new Canadians are not found among party members.

Canadian parties are not alone in having memberships that are not representative of the broader electorate. Recent studies in the United

Kingdom and Ireland find similar patterns. In both countries, membership is dominated by middle-aged and older men from the middle classes. For example, two-thirds of British Labour and Irish Fine Gael members are men. Half of British Conservative members are over sixty-five years of age, and in all three parties there are few young members (Seyd and Whiteley 1992; Whiteley, Seyd, and Richardson 1994; Gallagher and Marsh 2002). Parties in several Western democracies are facing similar crises of participation and inclusiveness at least in terms of their grassroots members.

Given that party members as a group do not reflect the sociodemographic makeup of Canadian society, it is interesting to consider the parties' attitudes toward inclusiveness in party decision making, which vary markedly. In the 1970s and 1980s the parties paid a good deal of attention to this issue. Within the three parties of the day (Liberal, Conservative, and NDP) there was support for efforts to increase the participation rates of women, youth, and new Canadians. As a result, the parties created internal structures with the aim of encouraging and facilitating the participation of these underrepresented groups. The Liberals and New Democrats continue to organize themselves in ways that attempt to ensure that a diverse coalition of interests is represented within their decision-making bodies.

The NDP's constitution provides, for example, for representation on the national executive of several constituent party groups, including the Participation of Women Committee, NDP Youth of Canada, the Participation of Visible Minorities Committee, and the Lesbian, Gay and Bisexual Committee. These committees are all charged with encouraging participation of underrepresented groups of Canadians within the party and to ensure that their interests are reflected in party decision making. For example, the Participation of Women Committee is mandated "to assist and encourage women's participation in all forms of political activity." Similarly, the Liberal Party has a standing committee on multiculturalism, an Aboriginal People's Commission, a Women's Commission, a Seniors' Commission, and a group called the Young Liberals of Canada. These efforts may partially explain why the memberships of these two parties are closer to gender parity, and generally more representative of Canadian society, than their opponents' members.

By contrast, the Conservatives moved away from this practice of differentiated membership in the 1990s, following the lead of the Canadian Alliance. The Alliance (and its predecessor the Reform Party) explicitly rejected this approach from its very beginning. Consistent with its populist impulses, the party sees individuals as the legitimate political unit and rejects group-based politics. The Alliance argues that there are not particular women's or youth or immigrant issues, but rather only Canadian issues. The party believes that the recognition of constituent groups of members would only further encourage a politics of special interests. Consequently the Alliance has regularly refused to establish a youth wing, women's organizations, or multicultural groups, although this does not mean the party is uninterested in attracting members from these groups. Indeed, some of its leading figures are women (for example, former deputy leader Deborah Grey and leadership candidate and long-time MP Diane Ablonczy), youth (including high-profile MPs Jason Kenney and Rob Anders), and visible minorities (such as veteran MP Rahim Jaffer). The point is that the party refuses to establish internal groups specifically aimed at advancing particular group-defined interests in party decision making.

With the exception of the Liberals, the parties' memberships do not reflect Canada's linguistic duality. Overall, approximately 20 percent of party members are francophone, 70 percent are anglophone, and 10 percent have another language as their mother tongue. The parties differ substantially in this regard. Virtually all members of the Bloc are francophones. Of the other four parties, only in the Liberal membership is there substantial representation of the francophone community, at 28 percent compared with 23 percent of the general population. Only 1 percent of Alliance members, 4 percent of New Democrats, and 6 percent of Conservatives claim French as their mother tongue. These numbers reflect the extreme regionalization of the Canadian party system. The Liberal Party is the only party with meaningful support in both francophone and anglophone Canada. Bloc members are, of course, concentrated in the province of Quebec; Alliance members are found mostly in western Canada and Ontario; the Conservatives are strongest in Atlantic Canada and Ontario; and the New Democrats enjoy pockets of support in western Canada, Ontario, and Nova Scotia.

The federal linguistic imbalance can be contrasted with the situation in New Brunswick, Canada's only officially bilingual province. The two principal provincial parties, the Conservatives and Liberals, each enjoy substantial representation in their membership ranks from both language groups (Cross and Stewart 2002). This situation is the result of a strong, affirmative effort on the part of both parties to win support from all segments of the electorate. Such an effort is more likely to occur in a two-party system than one with the substantial fragmentation found at the federal level. Indeed, convention delegate surveys suggest that both the Liberals and Conservatives managed substantial representation from both language groups before 1993, when the federal party system was far less fragmented than it is today.

Why Do Members Join?

What motivates the small proportion of voters who do join political parties? We asked members what their reasons were for originally joining their party, and as illustrated in Table 2.2, found that agreement

Table 2.2

Members' reasons for joining a political party

	Not at all important (%)	Somewhat important (%)	Very important (%)
To support a candidate for the local nomination	28	27	45
To support a candidate for party leader	38	26	36
I believe in the party's policies	3	14	84
I thought it would help my career	88	9	4
A friend asked me to	81	13	6
A family member asked me to	81	12	7
I thought it would help me get a government job	95	3	2
I wanted to influence party policy on an issue	44	37	19

with a party's policy positions is the most important factor. There is, however, significant variance between parties in this regard. Members of the more ideological parties, the Alliance and Bloc, are more likely to be motivated by support for their party's policies than are partisans of the traditional brokerage parties. This likely results from the clearer and more consistent policy positions staked out by the non-brokerage parties (for more on incentives to party membership, see Young and Cross 2002a).

Interestingly, while support for the party's policy positions is ranked very important by most members, fewer than one in five joined their party in an effort to influence the party's policy on a particular issue. This may be a reflection of their perception that regular members do not have much influence over party policy – a proposition considered in Chapter 3. This finding is consistent with voters' view that joining an interest group is a more effective method of influencing public policy than is belonging to a political party.

It is clear from Table 2.2 that leadership and nomination contests are important events that induce voters to join parties. Approximately seven in ten members claim to have originally joined a party in order to support either a preferred leadership or nomination candidate – comparable with the proportion that were motivated by support for the party's policy positions. It thus appears that nomination and leadership races are important triggers of the decision to join a party and that recruitment of members is largely limited to that group of voters who believe in a party's policy positions. And this survey does not include those voters who joined for one of these contests and subsequently withdrew from party membership. (Recruitment practices during nomination and leadership contests are explored further in Chapters 4 and 5.)

In order for the parties to be participatory institutions, they must not only attract members but must also manage to keep them. Accordingly, we asked members to tell us in their own words what they enjoy about belonging to parties. Support for the party's policies was, by far, the number-one answer. Only one-fifth as many members mentioned opportunity to influence either a party's decision making or policy

positions. This, again, is consistent with voters' perception that participation in parties is not a particularly effective way of influencing
public or party policy.

What Members Do

Even the most committed partisans who belong to the parties between
election campaigns are not very active in party affairs. While there are
differences between parties, most members spend little or, in many
cases, no time on party activity. A majority of members spend less
than one hour per month on party activity, and four in ten attended no
party functions in the year prior to being surveyed. It is noteworthy
that members of the New Democratic and Alliance parties, which prefer to present themselves as grassroots-driven, mass-membership parties, are very inactive, with relatively few spending any time on party
activity in the average month.

   Members of the Liberal Party are by far the most active (Table 2.3).
One-third of Liberals commit more than five hours a month to party
business, compared with an average of one member in ten in the
other parties. Similarly, one in four Liberals attended more than ten
party functions in the year prior to the survey, compared with one in
twenty in the other parties. While we might suspect that this results
from there being many more Liberal associations with an incumbent
MP than there are in the other parties, this does not appear to be the
case. Participation rates among Alliance and Liberal members do not
vary by region. Alliance members from the four westernmost
provinces, where the party holds a large majority of the seats in the
House of Commons, are just as inactive as Alliance members in the
rest of the country. Among western Alliance members, one in two
devotes no time in the average month to party affairs. Similarly, Liberal members in western Canada, where the party has few MPs, are as
active as their counterparts in Ontario, where the party holds virtually every seat.

Table 2.3

Participation of members in party activity

Time per month	Bloc Québécois (%)	Canadian Alliance (%)	Liberals (%)	New Democrats (%)	Progressive Conservatives (%)
None	56	45	22	55	32
Less than 1 hour	16	26	15	20	24
3 hours or more	16	13	44	13	24

Table 2.4

Participation rates of members in various party activities

	Bloc Québécois (%)	Canadian Alliance (%)	Liberals (%)	New Democrats (%)	Progressive Conservatives (%)
Displayed an election sign	63	73	91	86	87
Contributed funds	87	89	84	93	93
Attended nomination meeting	59	58	88	78	84
Volunteered in election campaign	62	52	86	82	78
Attended a local party meeting	59	71	89	75	88
Served on local party executive	14	18	59	35	49

Those members who do participate in party affairs are primarily engaged in low-intensity activity. The most common activity engaged in by party members is the contributing of funds (Table 2.4). While this obviously comes at some financial cost, it takes virtually no time or effort. Similarly, having an election sign in one's yard (usually erected by the party's active volunteer corps) is a popular activity with little cost to the member. Members are significantly less likely to volunteer in election campaigns, serve on a local association's executive, or raise funds for their party. Members of the new parties, the Alliance and the Bloc, are again at the bottom end of the participation scale. Only about half of the members of these parties have volunteered in an election campaign and about one-third have never attended a local party meeting.

The newest members of the parties appear to be among the least active. Those who joined a party after 1993 are less likely than party members as a whole to have engaged in any of these activities. Certainly, they have had less opportunity, particularly for election-related activities. However, this trend applies even to the most generic activity: the newest members are almost 20 percent less likely to have attended a local party meeting than are party members as a whole.

Again, the Canadian parties are not unique in having a considerable number of inactive members. Both of Britain's principal parties have a large percentage of members (about half) who are essentially inactive in party affairs (Seyd and Whiteley 1992; Whiteley, Seyd, and Richardson 1994). Ireland's Fine Gael party members are more active and have membership participation rates resembling those of Canada's Liberal Party (Gallagher and Marsh 2002).

Are Members Satisfied?

In considering why members are not more active, it is necessary to consider their views on the participatory opportunities offered them within the parties. In response to the general question of whether they are satisfied with the role members play, we find significant differences between the parties. Overall two-thirds of party members express satisfaction. However, this result is driven by members of the Bloc Québécois and the Alliance, eight in ten of whom express satisfaction with their role. In the three traditional parties, members are close to evenly split on the question. This is curious, considering that the members of the two newest parties are among the least active.

Nine in ten members of all five parties agree that their party should do more to encourage local associations to discuss matters of public policy. Similarly, seven in ten agree that regular party members should play a greater role in developing their party's election platform. There appears to be a consistent view that being a member of a political party does not provide a satisfactory opportunity to influence a party's position on policy questions (this notion is pursued more fully in the next chapter). While members think they do not exert enough influence on policy questions, approximately one in two party members believes that pollsters have too much influence.

Another way to address this question is to consider the amount of influence members feel various actors have in their party and to compare this with the amount of influence they believe the same actors should have. This comparison shows that members in all five parties believe that riding associations and ordinary members have less influence than they should have, pollsters have more influence than they should have, and party leaders have about the right amount.

As shown in Table 2.5, there are significant differences on these questions among parties. Liberals believe they, and their riding associations, have comparatively less influence than members of other parties believe they have within their parties. This may result from the Liberal Party being in government. A long-standing political truth holds that the closer a party comes to government, the tighter the concentration is of those exercising power. As the Liberals become entrenched in government, this suggests that power will become more highly concentrated among the party's elites. Consistent with this, the members of opposition "protest" parties (the Alliance and Bloc) that are ambivalent about governing believe they exercise the most influence within their parties.

Table 2.5

Members' views on influence various actors have and should have in party decision making

	Leader	Riding associations	Ordinary members	Pollsters
Influence actor *actually* has				
BQ	5.72	4.50	3.84	4.47
CA	5.97	4.67	4.59	4.17
Liberal	6.32	3.81	3.17	5.12
NDP	5.86	4.12	3.41	4.68
PC	5.97	4.25	3.59	5.00
Influence actor *should* have				
BQ	5.73	5.35	5.34	3.05
CA	5.59	5.14	5.61	2.78
Liberal	5.69	5.12	5.05	3.33
NDP	5.48	5.06	5.28	3.02
PC	5.84	5.24	5.01	3.13

Note: Figures based on scale of 1 to 7, with 1 being very little influence and 7 very influential, mean scores reported.

In each party, ordinary members are the group identified as having the largest differential in terms of comparing the influence they should have with the influence they actually have in party decision making. In each case, party members believe they should have substantially more influence. Members of all parties, except the Bloc, believe that leaders have slightly more influence than they should have.

Evaluating Party Membership

Canadian democracy requires a great deal from its political parties, and not all of these responsibilities are necessarily compatible with one another. As discussed in Chapter 1, one of the ongoing tensions has been between the views of grassroots activists, who prefer to see parties as vehicles for mass participation, and traditional expectations of brokerage and accommodation. As Canadians have become less deferential to elites and have come to prefer more direct participation in public life, their confidence in the traditional means of accommodative politics, including the old-line parties, has declined accordingly. The data presented in this chapter give us a better understanding of the contours of voter dissatisfaction with parties.

These data make clear that our parties are not highly participatory organizations. Few Canadians belong to them and most of these members are not regularly active in party affairs. Neither are the parties inclusive. Women, youth, and new Canadians are significantly under-represented. In terms of responsiveness, the parties face a double-edged sword. Grassroots members do not feel the central parties are responsive to them. Yet, if they were, the parties would rightly be accused of being captive to a narrow group of partisans who are representative of neither their own voters nor Canadians at large. For example, it would seem highly problematic to have party members determine child care or immigration policy considering their sociodemographic profile. Similarly, given the linguistic and regional imbalance found in the memberships of all but the Liberal Party, the memberships' capacity to deal with issues of regional and linguistic accommodation is suspect.

This is, of course, something of a chicken and egg dilemma. As long as membership in a political party is not seen as an effective way of influencing public decision making, few Canadians are likely to decide to become active party members; equally, as long as few Canadians join, party elites are on solid ground in arguing that their memberships are ill-equipped to settle policy issues in a way that fulfills their brokerage responsibilities. Nonetheless, given the centrality of parties to our politics, and the key roles they play in setting policy agendas, selecting candidates and leaders, and orchestrating election campaigns, if they are not inclusive and participatory it is difficult to imagine how our politics can be considered inclusive, participatory, and responsive to the views of Canadians. In the next chapter the focus is on the role members play in policy study and development. Not surprisingly, given the evidence presented thus far, members are generally dissatisfied with what they perceive to be elite-dominated policy processes within most of the parties.

Chapter 2

Party Membership in Canada

Strengths

- The parties are easily accessible to voters through constituency associations found in communities across the country.
- The parties put few restrictions on membership, allowing even those too young to vote and noncitizens to join.
- Almost all members have engaged in some party activity.
- Considerable membership recruitment surrounds leadership selection and candidate nomination contests.

Weaknesses

- Very few Canadians belong to political parties.
- Party members are not representative of Canadian society.
- Many members spend very little time on party activity.
- New members are among the least active.
- Members (and voters generally) do not see membership in a party as an effective way of influencing either party decision making or public policy.

POLICY STUDY AND DEVELOPMENT   3

Canadian parties have long seen their primary role as being electoral machines. The extraparliamentary parties exist to choose candidates and leaders and to help them get elected to the provincial and federal legislatures. Between elections, these party organizations have never been particularly active in developing policy options. The lack of a significant role for party members in policy development may help to explain the sharp decline in party membership routinely experienced between elections, the increased attractiveness of interest groups to those Canadians interested in influencing public policy, and the general dissatisfaction of many partisans with the operations of their own party.

Though this disenchantment was particularly strong in the final years of the twentieth century, it is not a recent phenomenon in Canadian politics. For almost a hundred years, party activists have made repeated efforts to win a more influential role in policy making. These demands will continue to brew and occasionally reach a boiling point, and they will continue to be frustrated, so long as the political parties have minimal interest in, and capacity for, interelection policy development. This chapter is concerned with two related subjects. The first is the role of grassroots members in party policy making, and the second is the parties' capacity for long-term policy study and development.

Members and Party Policy Development

Canadian parties have traditionally taken the approach that policy making is a function of the parliamentary party, with only a weak advisory role assigned to the extraparliamentary membership. The tensions between the membership party and the parliamentary group over policy making have usually been sharpest when a party is in government. Setting party policy during these periods is more meaningful because the party has the levers of the state at its disposal. Governing parties, cognizant of the disparate political interests that they must accommodate, have argued that the cabinet and parliamentary caucus are the only bodies capable of brokering all of the varied interests into a coherent public policy. Opposition parties are freer to advocate the more narrow interests of their activist membership bases, as they are not charged with governing. As a result, opposition parties are often responsive to the policy views of their members only to become substantially less so upon assuming the reins of government. Understandably, this often leads to a frustrated and dispirited party membership.

This cycle has a long history in Canadian politics. The federal Liberal Party in the first half of the last century provides a good example. Finding itself in opposition, the party held a national convention in 1919 to engage its activists in policy discussion and to select a successor to Wilfrid Laurier as party leader (the convention had initially been called for purposes other than leadership selection). The party subsequently won the general election of 1921 and spent most of the next twenty-seven years in government under the leadership of Prime Minister Mackenzie King. While in office, the government ignored many of the policies adopted by the 1919 meeting, and King never once called the party together in convention. During this long period of Liberal Party rule, the party's grassroots supporters had virtually no opportunity to exert themselves in the policy field. King believed that policy making was solely within the purview of the parliamentary party. The strength of his conviction is apparent in the following passage from a 1948 speech:

The substitution, by force or otherwise, of the dictates of a single
political party for the authority of a freely elected Parliament is
something which, in far too many countries, has already taken
place. It is along that path that many nations have lost their
freedom. That is what happened in Fascist countries. A single
party dictatorship, is likewise, the very essence of Communist
strategy (quoted in Wearing 1981, 74-5).

The contemporary Liberal and Conservative parties, the only parties to have governed federally, occasionally hold policy conventions at
which their members debate and adopt policy positions, but these are
in no way binding upon the parliamentary parties. Typically, these
processes are ad hoc and not part of an ongoing policy development
structure. The result is that their impact is often short-lived and negli-
gible. For example, after its second straight majority victory in 1988,
the Conservative government decided to engage its party membership
in a policy-making process to produce ideas for what it hoped would
be a continuing run in government. A rather elaborate process was
put into place with policy resolutions working their way up through
riding-level, regional, and provincial party meetings before appearing
on the agenda at a 1991 national policy conference. In total, 320 resolutions reached the national meeting out of more than 800 initially submitted by riding associations.

While party members may have thought they were setting the
future direction for the government this was clearly not the case. For
example, immediately after the convention delegates voted in favour
of privatizing the CBC, Communications Minister Perrin Beatty told
the press that he opposed the resolution and that the government had
no plans to follow the membership's directive. More importantly, there
was no follow-up to the policy process. Typical of the Canadian practice,
there was no permanent party body in place charged with policy study.
Consequently the work of the party members in debating and adopting these policy resolutions was forgotten almost as soon as the convention adjourned. Within short order, Prime Minister Brian Mulroney
resigned the party's leadership and the new leader, Kim Campbell,

appeared to give no particular regard to the recent policy process in setting out her platform for the subsequent general election. Instead the platform was largely devoid of specific policy planks and written by a few senior aides working for the leader. This scenario is characteristic of governing parties.

Governing parties have, however, occasionally tried to provide a significant role in policy making for their grassroots activists. The best example of such an effort at the federal level occurred in the first Trudeau government, from 1968-72. Upon coming to office the Trudeau Liberals set out several reforms aimed at providing an important role for their local partisans. These included a year-long constituency-level discussion of policy papers, a 1970 policy convention at which party members were to adopt policy resolutions uncontrolled by caucus or cabinet, regular reporting by cabinet ministers on the policies adopted by their ministries subject to a vote of approval by the membership in convention, and a promise that resolutions passed in convention would be included in the next election platform (this process is well described in Clarkson 1979).

The participatory enthusiasm of the late 1960s that encouraged these reforms quickly turned into the reality of governing and ultimately they had little impact. For example, instead of having individual ministers report on behalf of their departments and allowing for debate on each report, Trudeau quickly adopted the practice of presenting one report himself on behalf of the government. The result was that any criticism would be interpreted as a direct assault on the party leader. Similarly, the government rejected many of the key policy positions adopted at the 1970 convention. Stephen Clarkson sums up the subsequent disenchantment of party members:

> When it became clear that none of their policy positions would be adopted for the 1972 election campaign platform the morale of the party core fell noticeably. A survey of the most active Liberals in Ontario showed that it had been far harder to recruit volunteers in the 1972 election than it had been in 1968 and that campaign workers' morale had been far worse even in

constituencies that successfully returned a Liberal member of parliament (Clarkson 1979, 159).

Opposition parties have occasionally had more success with finding an influential role for their members. The federal Liberal Party under the leadership of Lester Pearson in the early 1960s and the Ontario Progressive Conservative Party under the leadership of Mike Harris in the 1990s both used periods in opposition to consult widely on policy consideration, to engage both their membership and outside experts in the process, and to use the process to define a set of policy options for their subsequent years in government. Both were former long-term governing parties that looked forward to returning to government and used their time in opposition to prepare for that eventuality.

The story of the Liberals in the 1960s is well known. Finding itself in opposition after nearly four decades in government, the party used the period between the 1958 and 1962 elections to develop a policy platform for its return to government. The highlight of this period was the party's 1960 Kingston conference, attended by 200 or so academics, party officials, and others with an interest in social, economic, and foreign policy. The conference sparked much policy discussion within the party, particularly around Tom Kent's call for a strengthened social welfare package. The following year the party held a much larger rally attended by close to 2,000 party activists, at which these and other policy ideas were debated and adopted in preparation for the 1962 election. Some key members of the future Liberal government, such as Walter Gordon, were brought into the party during this policy development period, and much of the policy agenda pursued in the first years of the Pearson government can be traced back to this period in opposition. However, once well established in government, the party reverted to form. Within days of a 1966 national convention, Pearson repudiated several of the policies adopted and "in spite of what the party's constitution now said he declared that the convention's resolutions did not establish party policy" (Wearing 1981, 75).

The case of the Ontario Conservatives in the 1990s is similar. After becoming leader of a then third-place party, Mike Harris authorized a party commission to travel the province, speaking to both party activists and policy experts, and to begin developing the foundation of a policy platform for a new Conservative government. The party later held a convention at which the results of this consultation were reviewed and adopted as party policy. (For more on this, see Cameron and White 2000). The "Common Sense Revolution" platform that the party successfully promoted in the 1995 election, and subsequently implemented during its first term in government, was the product of this policy development exercise.

The Bloc Québécois, Canadian Alliance, and New Democratic parties have argued for a more consistently influential role for their membership in policy development. In all three parties, official policy positions are determined by the membership at regular policy conventions and not by the parliamentary caucus. For the most part, the parliamentary party is meant to follow the policy direction established by the membership party. For example, the federal NDP's constitution includes the provision, "The convention shall be the supreme governing body of the Party and shall have final authority in all matters of federal policy, program and constitution" (Constitution of the New Democratic Party of Canada 2003, Article V, section 2).

This reflects the populist traditions of these parties and the fact that they are less interested in the practice of brokerage politics than are the Liberals and Conservatives. Of course none of these parties has come close to forming a government at the federal level. Since they all represent rather narrow ideological (and regional) spectrums and have shown little real interest in expanding their ideological bases, it is easier for them to cater to the views of their activists than it is for brokerage parties seeking to govern and maintain large, diverse coalitions.

However, even these newer parties, when forming governments at the provincial level, have struggled with providing a meaningful policy role for their members. The New Democrats experienced this difficulty in Ontario in 1990. Not expecting to win the upcoming election, the party entered the campaign with a policy platform reflecting the positions taken by its membership in convention. Having never before governed, the party had long argued it was more "democratic" than its Liberal and Conservative opponents by virtue of taking its policy directions from its grassroots supporters. Once elected, the party quickly realized that it was now charged with representing the whole province and not simply the views of its partisan base of social activists and trade union members. The party moved far away from the policy preferences of its members on issues such as a provincially run automobile insurance scheme, and implemented its social contract provisions, which were wildly unpopular with organized labour. The NDP was widely criticized by its members for breaking with the party tradition of having the legislative caucus follow the policy views of the members. That had been relatively easy to do in opposition but very difficult in government. The Parti Québécois has experienced similar tensions during its recent terms in power. The party's activist corps is more committed to the sovereignty cause than is the population at large. PQ governments, representing the entire electorate, are forced into a very delicate dance of keeping their committed activists satisfied while reflecting the views of the general populace.

Parties without an ongoing capacity for policy development find it far more difficult to engage their members in policy-related activities while in government. When it comes to taking policy direction from their activist members, from a democratic perspective this may be a good thing. Governments are charged with being responsive to all citizens. And surely, there is merit to the accommodative approach that Canadian governments at the federal level have always attempted to take. Party activists are often more extreme in their views (on both the left and the right) than are each parties' voters, and certainly more so than the electorate at large (see Cross and Young 2002). Governing parties have used this rationale to deny their members significant influence in policy setting.

The cost of this behaviour is the growing antipathy found among members toward a policy development process that they view as elite dominated and nonresponsive. As recounted in Chapter 2, members of every federal party believe they have less influence in party decision making than they should. A survey following the 1993 election found that in half of local Conservative and one-third of Liberal constituency associations, members had been offered no opportunity in the prior year for policy discussion. Not surprisingly, more than eight in ten local associations were dissatisfied with the opportunities provided them in this regard (Cross 1998). Similarly, the 2000 party member survey found that three-quarters of members believe they should play a greater role in developing their party's policy positions.

The challenge is to find a meaningful role for party members while preserving the parliamentary parties' responsibility for determining the ultimate policy positions. Turning policy making over to a party's members will not result in an inclusive and responsive politics for the citizenry at large. Instead, a better approach is for the parties to invest in policy study and development on an ongoing basis, to include a wide array of views in these processes, and over time to build an ideological foundation for their party on which subsequent shorter-term policies can be based.

The Royal Commission on Electoral Reform and Party Financing (1991, 1:292) captured the status of policy development in Canada's parties when it concluded, "The dilemma is that the core of the party organization is concerned primarily with elections; it is much less interested in discussing and analyzing political issues that are not connected directly to winning the next election, or in attempting to articulate the broader values of the party." In fact, most Canadian parties have essentially no capacity for ongoing policy study. Parties routinely lay off most of their staff immediately after each election and engage in little other than fundraising and housekeeping activities until the time arrives to begin preparation for the next election. This does not reflect the preferences of party members. As described earlier, those members who remain in the parties between elections, regardless of party affiliation, overwhelmingly say that they would like more party-sponsored opportunity for policy study and discussion. And this says nothing about the large majority of Canadians who choose not to belong to the parties and who, by a large margin, view participation in interest groups as a more effective way of influencing policy outcomes.

Party Policy Foundations

Unlike parties in some Western democracies, Canadian parties do not have policy institutes. Many European parties have either formal party institutes devoted to long-term policy study, or close ties with quasi-independent institutes committed to policy development. These organizations allow parties to engage their supporters in the policy process, to establish networks of policy experts, and to develop policy frameworks consistent with each party's overarching ideology. Of course, the operation of party policy institutes is costly, which is one reason Canadian parties have not established them. Many Canadian parties, particularly those in opposition, survive on shoestring budgets between elections. Parties routinely emerge from a general election campaign with a sizeable debt and spend the next years raising funds to pay it off before the next election brings another spending binge. Dollars are scarce during these periods and, even if they wanted to (which has not often been the case), parties simply have not had the funds necessary to engage in serious policy study work.

Other Western democracies have shown their commitment to party policy development by providing annual public funding to parties between elections. This is the case in many European countries including Austria, France, Germany, Italy, the Netherlands, and Sweden. A few provinces (including Quebec, New Brunswick, and Prince Edward Island) do provide modest annual funding to their parties, but these are the exception in Canada. All Canadian jurisdictions allocate annual funding to party caucuses represented in the respective legislatures. These funds, however, are restricted to the parliamentary party and encourage a policy development process that is both elite driven and focused on the short term. Party caucuses are understandably concerned with the cut and thrust of daily parliamentary debate and are not regularly engaged in longer-term policy study. The 2003 campaign finance legislation (reviewed in Chapter 7) changes this situation by providing the federal parties significant annual allowances of public money. What remains unclear is whether any of the parties will use this new funding to enhance their policy capacity.

Although Canadian parties typically do not have their own policy institutes, there are independent groups devoted to the study of public policy. These include the CD Howe Institute and the Fraser Institute on the right, the Canadian Centre for Policy Alternatives and the Caledon Institute of Social Policy on the left, and the Institute for Research on Public Policy in the centre. The traditional governing parties, the Liberals and Progressive Conservatives, have no history of formal or even quasi-formal ties with any of these groups. This differs from the situation in the United States. While the US parties themselves have limited policy-making capacity, both the Democrats and Republicans have forged close ties with groups of policy think-tanks on the left and right that essentially fill this void (Thunert 2003).

In the Conservatives' post-1993 restructuring efforts, a party task force proposed creating a permanent policy foundation to act as "a mechanism for Party member and riding level involvement in, and input to, the policy process" (Progressive Conservative Party 1994, 3). The party approved this proposal and committed itself in its new constitution to developing "a continuous policy process and a permanent policy resource which respects and encourages the participation of members." The party never acted on this commitment.

Two Canadian parties have moved in the direction of increasing their capacity for policy study and development. The Canadian Alliance has established close relationships with groups on the right of centre, including the National Citizens Coalition (NCC), the Canadian Taxpayers Federation (CTF), and the Fraser Institute. The party's current leader, Stephen Harper, is a former president of the NCC and veteran caucus members such as Jason Kenney, formerly with the CTF, have close ties with these groups. The NDP is the one federal party to have created a formal connection with a policy foundation, the Douglas-Coldwell Foundation. While the foundation is formally independent of the party, the connections are apparent in the makeup of its board of directors, which has included former NDP premiers Alan Blakeney and Howard Pawley, high-profile MP Bill Blaikie, and former NDP federal secretaries Jill Marzetti and David Woodbury. The foundation played an important role in the policy renewal conferences the party held following its electoral devastation in 1993.

Party policy institutes, or the development of strong ties with quasi-independent groups, are a vehicle for serious, ongoing policy study and development. This activity provides many benefits to parties and to democracy generally. Five of the principal advantages of policy institutes are listed below.

1 Policy institutes provide a way for parties to engage their members in the policy development process. The data recounted above unequivocally show party members' dissatisfaction with their current role in this process.
2 Policy institutes generate policy alternatives for parliamentary parties to consider. Policy debate currently is dominated by the parliamentary parties, which have little capacity to develop new, detailed policy positions.
3 Policy institutes can assist a party in making the transition from opposition to government. Virtually overnight the task of the parliamentary leadership changes from one of primarily criticizing the government to identifying and implementing a policy plan. A party institute can help by preparing detailed policy alternatives for the new government's consideration.
4 Policy positions can be re-examined and alternatives considered without drawing the same intensity of media attention and public scrutiny that inevitably results when such ruminations come from a parliamentary party. Parliamentary parties are loath to reconsider their positions for fear of a public perception that they are backtracking on their promises or of acknowledging that they were misguided in the first place. Policy institutes can provide the space for such deliberation, some distance removed from a party's immediate political imperatives.
5 Institutes can serve to develop a network of experts engaged in advising the party on long-term policy direction. This is somewhat less partisan an activity than advising a parliamentary

party on the immediate issues of the day, and can involve more academics and other serious students of public policy. Parties can also use this process to reach out to areas, regional and otherwise, where they have limited electoral support.

A party foundation also addresses one of the common arguments made against effective grassroots participation in party policy making in the Canadian context. The argument, as made by Prime Minister King, is that political parties need to be responsive to all voters, and not solely their activist base. Consequently they cannot take their policy direction solely from the views of their own supporters. This argument is most often made by the traditional brokerage parties; both the Conservatives and Liberals regularly maintain that they have to broker the wide array of interests found in Canada, accommodate the disparate views, and try to find common ground. A party-run policy foundation can be useful to a brokerage party by focusing party members' participation into the foundation and thereby providing otherwise frustrated members with opportunity to participate in policy study and development. Channelling this participation into a policy foundation provides some necessary distance between the policy demands of the party's activist corps and its parliamentary party. The parliamentary party benefits from the policy work of the foundation but is ultimately free to set its own course.

A well-run foundation also ensures that voices beyond the party's own members are considered in framing policy objectives. This may be particularly valuable in Canada, where all of the federal parties have large areas of regional electoral weakness and thus gaping holes in regional representativeness in their parliamentary caucuses (and often in their grassroots membership). Of course, member participation through policy institutes does not ensure responsiveness. The parliamentary parties will not always follow the direction of their party members. And the parliamentary party itself, particularly when in government, does not always play the definitive role in policy making. As mentioned in Chapter 1, some have observed a significant concentration of policy-making authority within the prime minister's office in recent years (Savoie 1999; Simpson 2001).

Ironically, given the brokerage parties' reluctance to establish policy foundations, an argument can be made that parties are disadvantaged in fulfilling the brokerage function by a lack of capacity for policy innovation. Groups that are not represented in the parliamentary party (or in the prime minister's office) find it difficult to have their interests heard in the closed world of party caucuses and cabinet meetings. When party policies (and government policy) are made largely in a vacuum by a small group of party elites, interests not represented in that group may be shut out (Brodie and Jenson 1991). For example, Westerners argued that there was no place for their policy preferences to be considered in the later Trudeau governments, which included almost no MPs from western Canada. When outside interests are heard, they often come in the form of representations from single-interest groups not concerned with compromise and accommodation. Policy foundations could ensure that voices are heard from all regions and segments of society and at their best could generate alternative policy proposals for consideration by the party's parliamentary leadership.

Policy foundations also serve, in the long term, to give parties a clearer ideological imprint and to bring some continuity to a party's policy direction. Canada's parties are dominated by the personalities of their leaders. Leaders typically exercise substantial control over candidate selection, election campaigning, and policy adoption. Election campaigns largely revolve around the leader and are orchestrated by a small team of his or her close personal advisors. Because the policy direction a party takes is largely determined by the preferences of its leader, it is often difficult to ascribe characteristics to the party independent of its current leader. And too often leaders and their operatives, in search of electoral success, avoid staking out specific policy positions for fear of alienating groups of voters (for more on this, see Clarke et al. 1996).

Strengthening Party Policy Development

In arguing for a stronger policy development capacity for parties, Robert Young has written:

> In a self-reinforcing cycle, people with genuine policy concerns
> seek out interest groups to advance their causes, and the parties
> degenerate further into domination by leaders and their per-
> sonal entourages, who play the politics of image and strategic
> vagueness, who take office with little sense of direction, and
> who end up as brokers among interest groups (Young 1991, 77).

In this scenario, parties end up responding to special- and single-interest groups because these often have greater capacity for policy development than do the parties themselves. All parties and governments eventually need to take policy positions, and if they do not have the capacity to engage both experts and the general citizenry in the policy development process then they are reduced to responding to proposals made by organized interests.

This situation is particularly unsatisfactory in a country with a long tradition of brokerage politics. Parliamentary parties in both government and opposition would benefit from serious study undertaken by their extraparliamentary parties toward providing policy alternatives and guidance to the parliamentary parties. Such activity would serve to encourage those Canadians with policy concerns to participate in party activity rather than looking to interest groups as a way to influence public policy. A beneficial side effect might also be a weakening of the growing concentration of government-party decision making within the prime minister's office.

While local party members play a limited role in policy development, they have traditionally been the central figures in candidate recruitment and selection. The evolving role of grassroots partisans in this key party function is the subject of the next chapter. Given that the legislative caucuses often play an important role in policy development, at the expense of the parties' grassroots members, the norms of candidate selection and the influence of local party members in the process take on added importance.

CHAPTER 3

Policy Study and Development

STRENGTHS

- ♀ Parties occasionally engage their memberships in formal policy development processes.
- ♂ The NDP has established the Douglas-Coldwell Foundation.
- ♀ The Alliance has developed close ties with several right-of-centre policy groups.
- ♂ Opposition parties have occasionally engaged in serious, long-term policy development in anticipation of the transition to government.

WEAKNESSES

- ♀ Most parties have neither a policy foundation nor strong ties with independent policy groups.
- ♂ Parties commit few resources to ongoing policy study.
- ♀ Members are generally dissatisfied with the opportunities for policy study and development afforded them.
- ♂ Voters see interest group involvement as a more effective means of influencing policy change than belonging to a political party.
- ♀ Policy making within governing parties is increasingly dominated by the prime minister's office.

CANDIDATE SELECTION

4

In locations as varied as school gymnasiums, hockey arenas, hotel ballrooms, fire halls, and church basements, political party members gather by the hundreds and sometimes thousands at the outset of each general election campaign. The central offices of the major political parties will have called upon their local constituency associations to choose the candidates for the upcoming election. Local activists select a location in their riding, set a date and time for the meeting, and accept nominations from would-be candidates. The candidates spend weeks and sometimes months travelling the riding talking to the party's supporters and organizing their friends and relatives to attend the nomination meeting and vote for them. At the chosen hour, the candidates' organizational skills are put to the test as they deliver their supporters to the voting site. Party members fill the hall wearing buttons and waving placards bearing the name of their preferred candidate. The candidates enter to great excitement among their supporters, speeches are given, and the balloting begins. The first candidate to receive a majority endorsement from those present is chosen the party's local candidate. The event usually concludes with a show of party unity as the defeated candidates and their supporters pledge to support the successful nominee. Thousands of kilometres separate these local events, many different languages are spoken, and local political and social cultures vary; nonetheless, the theatre of candidate nomination is similar across the country.

This is the portrait of candidate nomination commonly presented in the popular media and scholarly work, and indeed, it describes many nomination contests. This chapter examines how generally accurate this portrayal of a highly competitive, participatory, and localized process is today. Consideration of the candidate nomination process is an essential part of any examination of the democratic character of Canada's political parties. One of the principal functions of parties is the identification and recruitment of the men and women who serve in our legislative bodies. Unlike general elections, which are organized and governed by law, nomination contests have almost no state involvement. Rather, like leadership contests, they are organized by the political parties and therefore reflect the democratic norms and values present in the parties at any given time. The importance of the candidate nomination function of political parties was captured by Schattschneider (1942, 101) more than sixty years ago when he wrote, "The nominating process has become the crucial process of the party. He who can make the nominations is the owner of the party."

Primary Functions of Nomination

In this chapter, we are concerned with both the process and the outcomes of candidate nomination. Is the process an opportunity for participation, inclusiveness, and responsiveness in the choosing of a party's legislative candidates? How open is the process to potential candidates of different backgrounds and experiences? How representative are those nominated of the general electorate? The literature and practice of candidate nomination suggest that it serves four primary functions in our political process:

1   opportunity for widespread grassroots participation in party
    politics

2   opportunity for voters to choose the type of individual they wish to represent them in the legislature

3   socialization of new immigrant communities into Canadian politics

4   recruitment of elected representatives.

We begin with an introduction to each of these functions.

.   On the surface, candidate nomination processes appear to be the most accessible form of meaningful participation in a Canadian political party. Most voters will never travel to their provincial or national capitals to lobby elected members, attend a central party convention, or serve on a party's executive. Many, however, will help choose a local party candidate. Nominations take place in each of the country's 301 constituencies, and the decision on the choice of candidate is generally left to the discretion of the local party members. While the possibilities for meaningful, widespread voter participation are great, we will see that in practice candidate nomination processes actually pose substantial barriers to participation and that relatively few voters get involved.

Through the nomination process the parties select the men and women from among whom voters elect their members of Parliament and the provincial legislatures. It is nearly impossible to be elected without the endorsement of one of the major parties. For example, of the 602 victorious candidates in the federal elections of 1997 and 2000, only one was not a party nominee (and he had been a Liberal MP in the past). In this sense the parties serve as gatekeepers to elective office. Nomination contests afford the only direct opportunity for voters to express a preference for the individual they would like to have as their representative. In Canada's parliamentary system, voters only have one ballot during a general election. The result of this vote determines not only who will serve as their local representative, but also who will be prime minister and which party will form the government. (This can be contrasted with, for instance, the US system, where voters cast one ballot for their local representatives to Congress and a separate one for president, with many voting for candidates of differing parties for the two offices.)

Studies of voting behaviour suggest that voters' views on local party candidates are of only minor importance in determining whom to vote for in a general election, as voters are also concerned with the choice of a governing party. Nonetheless, the choice of a local representative is important. This person represents their community in the legislature, advocates for his or her constituents' interests within the party caucus, and serves as ombudsperson for them in the provincial or federal capital (for more on the various functions of the representative see Docherty 2004). The only time voters have an unencumbered opportunity to express their preference for a local representative is during the candidate nomination process. Nonetheless, this chapter concludes that nomination contests rarely offer voters the opportunity to deliberate and assess the policy views of the candidates or their qualities as potential ombudspersons, but rather are primarily contests of organizational capacity.

Nomination contests have traditionally offered a point of entry into the political process for new and underrepresented groups of Canadians. This has been especially true of immigrant communities. For example, in the twentieth century, members of the Ukrainian, Italian, and Irish communities were introduced to federal and provincial politics through participation in party nomination contests. Patterns of immigration have changed, but this phenomenon continues. Particularly in urban centres, nomination battles routinely feature significant mobilization of new immigrants, often in support of a candidate from their ethnic community. Members of the Indo-Canadian and Asian Canadian communities have been especially active in nomination contests at both the federal and provincial levels in recent years. Parties generally encourage these ethnic recruitment drives by having lenient rules for voting eligibility in nomination contests: Canadian citizenship is not required. The recruitment of new and non-Canadian party members has become highly controversial. The parties are under pressure from some of their long-time activists to reform nomination rules to make these types of mobilization efforts more difficult. Many of the ethnic community members mobilized to join parties during these contests do not continue as party members after the nomination is decided.

Because members of legislative assemblies are chosen almost exclusively from among the candidates nominated by the major parties, concern with the underrepresentation of women and minority groups within the legislatures must begin with consideration of the candidate nomination process. We will see in this chapter that the parties take dramatically different approaches in this regard. Some take a laissez-faire approach, arguing that party members have the prerogative to decide who they think will make the best candidate and representative without being encumbered by any affirmative action constraints. Others aggressively set targets for the numbers of candidates from particular groups to be nominated, and implement practices favouring candidates from these groups. While the parties are aware of the shortfall of women and visible minority candidates and have taken some steps to address it, much remains to be done.

Local versus Central Control

One of the key factors affecting each of the concerns set out above is the degree to which candidate nomination is a function of the local or central party. Those concerned about participation and responsiveness favour local control, where the selection is left to the parties' grassroots activists. Those concerned with inclusiveness (at least as it relates to the legislative caucus) look to the central party to establish rules and processes that favour candidates from underrepresented groups. The general rule in Canada is that candidate nomination is left to the discretion of local party members within a framework set by the central party. Carty, Cross, and Young (2000) refer to this as a trade-off in which candidate nomination is left to local associations in return for strict party discipline within the legislative caucus.

While this portrayal of candidate nominations suggests absolute local authority, there are many historical examples of central party involvement in nomination processes. In his study of the federal Liberal Party from 1930 to 1958, Reginald Whitaker (1977, 143) observes that candidate nomination meetings were often orchestrated events with regional ministers having significant influence over who the local candidates would be. In his study of Newfoundland politics, S.J.R. Noel (1971, 282) reports that from the time the province joined Confederation in 1949 until his leaving office in 1968, Premier Joey Smallwood had near-absolute control over federal party nominations in the province. Recent evidence suggests that central party involvement continues and may be more intrusive and pervasive than widely believed. For example, in survey data collected after the 1993 federal election one-third of Liberal associations reported outside interference by their national party in their selection of a candidate (Cross 2002a, 374). Of course, the very concept of "outside interference" implies that local autonomy remains the norm.

By statute, the central parties have the final say in naming candidates. In the lead-up to the 1972 federal election, the Canada Elections Act was amended to provide for the inclusion of party affiliation next to local candidates' names on the ballot (prior to this, the ballot contained the names and occupations of local candidates without any indication of party affiliation). Elections Canada officials were concerned that, in the event of more than one individual making a claim, they not be put in the position of having to determine who was a party's legitimate candidate. To avoid this scenario, a provision was included in the act requiring the party leader to endorse the party's candidate in each riding. This provision allows the central parties to pressure local associations to nominate a candidate of their liking.

Many of the restrictions placed on the local prerogative are rather benign attempts to ensure order and conformity in the process across the country and to make the timing of nominations consistent with the party's electoral strategy. These provisions typically include rules dictating the timing of nomination meetings, membership cut-off dates, a standard fee for participation, a minimum voting age, and guidelines for the participation of voters from outside a constituency. In recent decades some central parties have asserted themselves by setting rules that favour female and minority candidates, discourage participation by strongly ideological candidates, restrict participation by "undesirable" candidates (such as those facing criminal charges), and favour high-profile candidates.

Taking this authority even further, recent elections have seen Prime Minister Jean Chrétien appoint local Liberal candidates with minimal or no consultation with local party members. The mere threat of vetoing a chosen candidate or unilaterally appointing a candidate can also lead the local association to acquiescence to the preference of the central party. When Chrétien assumed the Liberal leadership, the party amended its constitution to give the leader absolute control over nomination contests. Candidate appointments are only one manifestation of this. Provincial campaign chairs (appointed by the prime minister) have regularly told would-be candidates that they were unacceptable to the party and should not seek the nomination or risk the public embarrassment of having the leader reject their nomination. Similarly, central party officials have occasionally rigged the process to ensure the nomination of a favoured candidate without having to resort to appointing a candidate.

A long-time Liberal MP and senior cabinet minister, Brian Tobin, concluded that the party's current rules governing candidate selection amount to "a massive shift of power from riding associations and provincial organizations to the national leader and the national campaign committee" (Winsor 1992). The Liberal Party has been much more active in this regard than any of the other parties, most of which have criticized Chrétien's appointment of candidates as "undemocratic." The balance of authority over candidate nomination between the central and local parties is considered throughout the discussion that follows.

Voter Participation

Evaluations of voter participation in candidate nominations depend on whether the observer chooses to see a glass that is half-full or half-empty. On the positive side, more voters participate in nominations than in any other party activity. As discussed in Chapter 2, membership in most Canadian parties increases dramatically during election periods and this is driven primarily by interest in nomination campaigns. On the negative side, only a minuscule proportion of general election voters participate in these contests.

The average attendance at the 1993 nomination meetings (the last year for which comprehensive data are available) in the Liberal, Conservative, and Reform parties was 413, and this number is greatly increased by a few associations with hotly contested and very large meetings. The median attendance was just 201, and one-third of associations had fewer than 100 voters participate (Cross 2002a, 378). In most ridings, four of the major parties nominate candidates; thus, it is likely that fewer than 1,000 voters participated in all of a riding's local nomination meetings combined. This represents less than 2 percent of the eligible voters in a riding. The evidence also suggests that only a minority of the parties' members participate in these contests (estimates range from one-third to one-half) (Cross 2002a, 379).

The number of voters participating in nomination contests appears to have decreased over time. More than a half-century ago, Dawson (1947, 444) observed that "a normal attendance is four or five hundred." While this number is modestly larger than today's average, the difference in participation rates is probably even greater because there were fewer voters in each riding fifty years ago. Also, those attending the nomination meetings at that time were often delegates chosen from subdivisions within the riding, meaning that many more party members participated in the selection of these nomination meeting delegates.

It is worth noting that in the United States, where candidate nominations are governed by statute, typically take place on a single date in each state, and are conducted in a manner identical to general elections, participation rates are considerably higher. As discussed further in Chapter 5, participation in the nomination contests for US presidential candidates in 2000 averaged approximately 20 percent of the electorate. Participation in congressional primaries ranges dramatically, but in contested elections often exceeds 10 percent.

Observers often bemoan what they consider low levels of participation in these contests. Nonetheless, the percentage of Americans voting in these candidate selection contests is considerably higher than Canadian participation in their counterparts.

For purposes of the Audit we are left with the question of why so few voters participate in these events. The primary reason may be that nominations, like leadership selection, are viewed as the private affairs of political parties. One must be a member, pay a membership fee, keep abreast of party activity, and attend a party meeting in order to participate. The barriers to participation are far higher than for voting in a general election.

In order to be able to participate in a nomination contest, voters must first join the party. This requires the payment of a membership fee (usually in the $10 to $25 range). Since, as discussed in Chapter 2, many members join for the sole purpose of participating in the nomination contest and have no intention of partaking in other party events, this is essentially a poll tax. Those unwilling or unable to pay the fee are disenfranchised from the nomination contest. It is difficult to know just how many voters are deterred by these fees. Though many parties formally prohibit such practices, it is widely believed that candidates and their supporters often pay the fee for any potential voters who hesitate to join. Perhaps for this reason, only 2 percent of constituency association presidents believe the fee is a serious deterrent to participation (Cross 1996b, 172). Of course, those dissuaded from participating because of the poll tax may never come to the attention of the constituency presidents, since they never join the party.

Voters are also required to travel to one location in each riding and spend an average of two to three hours at the nomination meeting. This raises additional hurdles to participation. Many of Canada's rural ridings are geographically large. In these ridings, party members commonly have to travel a hundred or more kilometres to attend a nomination meeting. The time required to travel to and attend the meeting also requires a significant commitment and is, of course, more difficult for those with substantial family or work responsibilities. Candidates often use the choice of location to their strategic advantage. The

58

decision is usually made by the local party executive, and candidates planning ahead work to have their supporters placed on the executive so that they control these decisions. When there are candidates from different geographic locations in the riding, executive members supporting one candidate often vote to have the meeting in the home town or neighbourhood of their preferred candidate believing that he or she is likely to have more supporters in that local area.

These strategic calculations are not restricted to geographic considerations. The National Film Board documentary *The Right Candidate for Rosedale* (1979) presents a compelling portrait of the contest for the Liberal Party nomination in a federal by-election in the mid-1970s. Supporters of candidate John Evans, the favourite of the local party establishment, controlled the choice of voting location and selected the ballroom of a posh downtown Toronto hotel. Evans, then president of the University of Toronto, was supported by the party's local elites, who were accustomed to frequenting such places. His opponent was social worker Ann Cools. Cools built a solid support base among the lower economic classes in the riding – single mothers, the unemployed, and the generally disenfranchised. The film shows her supporters feeling intimidated about entering such a "swanky" location and worrying whether they have appropriate clothes for such a venue.

Parties also routinely require that voters join the party before a set cut-off date in order to vote in a nomination contest. These dates vary widely among parties and can range from seven to ninety days prior to the vote. Consequently the deadline for becoming eligible to vote in the nomination contest can pass before most voters even know that the contest is under way. Many nomination meetings occur before the dropping of the writ that marks the official beginning of the election campaign. During this pre-election period voters are unlikely to be following local party affairs (remember, very few Canadians actually belong to the parties between elections). Local media does not pay significant attention to nomination contests until closer to the day of the vote, when it is too late in many instances to join and become eligible to participate. As a result the voters who do participate tend to be the long-time party members who are part of the local party's communication networks, and the friends and supporters of candidates who are mobilized by them to participate. Other voters who may wish to have a say in the choice of their local candidate may well not know that the contest is taking place until after the membership deadline passes.

A further deterrent to voter participation is the fact that many nominations are uncontested. Not surprisingly, the participation rate in contested nominations is substantially higher than in those that are uncontested. For example, in 1993 the average attendance at a contested nomination meeting was 574 compared with 183 for uncontested races (Cross 2002a, 380). Three principal factors lead to a large number of uncontested nominations. First, the increased regionalization of the party system creates large areas of the country in which parties are not competitive. The parties often find it a challenge to recruit even a single candidate in these no-hope ridings. Second, the closed nature of nomination contests probably dissuades many would-be candidates in competitive ridings. Candidates with the greatest chance of winning a competitive nomination race are those with widespread support among a party's local activists and those with a strong organizational team prepared to mobilize large numbers of supporters. Those more interested in policy debates than organization-focused, intraparty tussles may well be turned off (thus the Liberal Party's recent tradition of appointing high-profile candidates, allowing them to bypass the unpleasantness of the nomination process). Finally, the norm is that incumbents not be challenged for renomination. About nine in ten incumbents seeking renomination typically face no opponent. The result is that the most desirable nominations (desirable because the party has shown a recent ability to win the riding and elect its nominee) are least likely to be contested.

While there are isolated cases in each campaign of an incumbent being challenged and losing a nomination, these are the exceptions that prove the rule. More typical of the treatment of incumbent candidates is Liberal leader Jean Chrétien's decree before his first campaign as party leader in 1993 that all Liberal incumbents be renominated without opposition. The central party went to great lengths to ensure

Chrétien's wishes were fulfilled, as illustrated in the following example. Len Hopkins was the incumbent Liberal member of Parliament for
an eastern Ontario riding. He had fallen out of favour with local party
activists and a move was afoot to draft a viable candidate to challenge
him for the nomination. Concerned that Hopkins might be vulnerable
to such a challenge, Liberal Party officials ensured there would be no
contest. In full compliance with the party's new rules, meant to give
the leader more authority over the nomination process, the party's
Ontario campaign chair declared nominations for the riding open one
morning from his Toronto office, then closed the nomination period
later that same day. He informed the riding association that the period
for nominations had come and gone and that Hopkins was the only
candidate to file the necessary papers. The local association was out-
raged but had no recourse under the party's rules.

The Liberal Party has not always gone through the motions of at
least formally following a set of rules (as in the Hopkins case) when
orchestrating the nomination of a preferred candidate. In the three
campaigns in which he led the party, Jean Chrétien unilaterally
appointed some candidates each time. This has been done often after
little consultation with local party activists and sometimes against
vocal and widespread dissatisfaction with the leader's interference in
what the party's grassroots supporters feel is their prerogative. Chrétien has justified these appointments as a way to ensure the nomination of more female candidates, block undesirable candidates, and
attract "star" candidates. Indeed, a majority of the appointed candidates have been women and many have been high-profile (including
cabinet ministers such as John McCallum, Art Eggleton, Jean Augustine, and Marcel Massé). There are, however, less intrusive methods of
encouraging the nomination of women short of taking the decision
completely away from the voters (some of these are discussed below).
One must also wonder why high-profile candidates need to be
appointed; surely their star quality would help them win a nomination
contest. As for undesirable candidates, the party regularly informs
candidate hopefuls that their nomination would be unacceptable and
that, should they be successful, their papers will not be signed by the

leader. Surely, undesirable candidates can be prevented from running (as they have been in all of the major parties) without the appointment of a particular candidate.

The Canadian Alliance has taken a different tack in this regard. There appears to be more tolerance for those wishing to challenge a sitting member for a nomination – more than one-fifth of Alliance MPs were challenged in their bids for renomination in 2000. The party has also taken the position that authority over nomination contests lies with the local activists and has interfered far less in these affairs than has the Liberal Party. The Alliance leadership has strongly criticized Jean Chrétien for his interference in Liberal nomination contests. The Alliance constitution includes a provision prohibiting its leader from using the statutory requirement to sign candidates' nomination papers as a way of influencing local contests. The party has, instead, vested this authority with its national council and used it sparingly. Consistent with its campaign rhetoric, in the case of candidate nomination, the Alliance appears to give primacy to concerns of participatory grassroots democracy.

The New Democrats have established an elaborate set of central party rules governing candidate nomination. Most of these are aimed at increasing the numbers of women and visible minorities nominated by the party. These provisions are considered later in this chapter.

Selecting a Representative

Grassroots participation in nomination contests is not simply a matter of how many voters participate. While numbers reflect the extent of participation, they say nothing about the quality of participation. Ideally, the process should allow local party members to assess the various merits of the candidates for the nomination, to consider these according to the traits they think important in a representative, and then to vote accordingly. In studying candidate nominations, I have attended nomination meetings, spoken with candidates for nomination, and on occasion accompanied them during their nomination campaign efforts, in most of the major parties and in different parts of the country. These experiences have taught me that the nomination process is rarely deliberative. Voters do not generally gather information about the various candidates, consider their policy positions and other qualifications, listen to the speeches at the nomination meetings and then decide whom to vote for. Rather, many, perhaps most, of those attending nomination meetings are friends, relatives, and associates of the candidates. They join the party and attend the meeting for the express purpose of supporting a particular nomination candidate, and may not even consider themselves supporters of the party. They arrive at the nomination meeting in a bus or carpool organized by the candidate who solicited their participation, knowing full well whom they will support, and never consider voting for a different candidate.

Long-time members of the party who have participated in many nomination contests often act differently from the new recruits described above. They toil in the party between election campaigns and give serious consideration to who would make the best candidate and representative. They are more likely to consider several different candidates before deciding whom to support. These truly grassroots party activists, however, often make up only a small percentage of those who actually attend and vote in contested nomination meetings (particularly in ridings a party is likely to win). In most parties, candidate nomination contests are about organization and voter mobilization. The successful candidate doesn't spend extensive time thinking about the kind of representation she will offer to the party, nor does she prepare detailed policy positions. Rather, campaign time is spent identifying and mobilizing as many supporters as possible to attend the nomination meeting. The appeals are often personal and made to friends and associates and to those with whom the candidate shares some common bond, such as membership in a particular ethnic community.

The New Democrats differ somewhat from the other parties in this regard. Membership in the NDP is considerably more stable in election and nonelection periods than in the other parties. The party has less of a tradition of signing up new members solely for the purpose of nomination contests, and consequently the core group of party activists is not routinely overwhelmed by new recruits at the nomination meeting. The Canadian Alliance also, while resembling the traditional parties in terms of voter mobilization in contested nomination races, places more emphasis on candidates' policy positions during the nomination contest. This may result from the party's expressed position that elected members should be less bound by party discipline than is the case in the older parties (it is not clear that this principle has much effect in practice, but it is widely supported among the party's grassroots supporters). Generally speaking, however, policy plays virtually no role in nomination campaigns and the parties often take steps to discourage it.

In their study of candidate nomination in the 1988 federal election, Carty and Erickson (1991, 122) conclude, "This is largely a portrait of a process typically neither disciplined nor driven by issues or distinctive social groups." Data collected after the 1993 election support this conclusion. Only one in four associations with contested nominations reported policy differences among the candidates, with no significant difference among the parties (Cross 2002a, 381). One reason may be that the process provides little opportunity for any policy differentiation to appear. Overall, in just half of associations with a contested nomination was there a debate between the candidates, and this number is greatly inflated by the frequent occurrence of debates in the Reform Party. Four-fifths of contested Reform nominations had a debate, compared with half that number in both the Liberal and Conservative parties.

Nevertheless, voters may prefer contests in which policy is discussed. In 1993 voter turnout at contested nomination contests was significantly higher both in contests with substantive policy differences between the candidates and in contests that included a candidate debate (Cross 2002a, 380-2). The timing of nomination contests, many of which occur before the official launch of the election campaign (80 percent according to Carty and Erickson 1991, 112), means that nomination contests often take place well before the campaign's key policy issues are determined. Similarly, voter interest in the campaign has yet to peak. Accordingly, those attending are the few committed party members and the hordes who are mobilized largely because of a personal commitment to a candidate.

The Liberal Party is clearly not interested in candidate nomination contests revolving around policy questions. When voters interested in specific issues have organized in an attempt to get one of their supporters nominated, the party has often acted to thwart the effort. For example, some of the candidate appointments made by Chrétien were for the express purpose of preventing the nomination of a candidate supported by the anti-abortion group Liberals for Life. These attempts by supporters of a particular policy position to control a nominating convention are often portrayed as illegitimate attempts to hijack the process. The argument is that these voters are not interested in the health of the party, but rather are looking for a vehicle to advance their own narrow policy positions. This argument ignores the reality that most voters at hotly contested nomination contests are newly recruited and are participating for reasons unique to that contest and not out of a general fondness for the party.

The Canadian Alliance seems less bothered by attempts to make individual policies a more important factor in nomination contests. Another anti-abortion group called Campaign Life Coalition organized to nominate like-minded candidates in the Alliance in the 2000 federal election. While the effort had mixed results, there was no institutional backlash in the party against this type of policy-based mobilization. Campaign Life's director Steve Jalsevac commented that the Alliance was much more open to this kind of activity, noting that in past similar efforts in the Conservative and Liberal parties, "the problem was those two parties didn't want open democracy" (Harper 2000).

Minority Group Inclusion

Consideration of inclusiveness in candidate nomination contests must include the issue of mobilization of large numbers of ethnic and

visible minorities into the parties to support a candidate. Because contested nomination contests revolve around efforts to recruit large
numbers of new or "instant" members, candidates seek out tightly
organized, hierarchical communities where winning the support of a
few community leaders can result in literally hundreds of supporters
from that community. For many decades candidates have found ethnic
minority communities to be ideal for these purposes. For example, in
the 1962 federal election, Howard Scarrow observed an extensive
recruitment drive in ethnic communities in the contest for the Liberal
nomination in the Ontario riding of Urban. Scarrow (1964) estimates
that three-quarters of the 1,200 voters in the contest were new Canadians. In the 2000 election campaign, membership in the Alliance association in the riding of Calgary Northeast skyrocketed to more than
15,000 from 450 in the previous election. The increase was due to a
hotly contested nomination contest in which several members of the
Sikh community, who were challenging incumbent MP Art Hanger in
his bid for renomination, pursued vigorous recruitment and mobilization strategies among the Sikh population in the riding. Observers
estimated that as many as two-thirds of the new members were Sikhs.

There are two competing views of this phenomenon. The first is
that mass mobilization of new residents of Canada – many of whom
may not be citizens and thus are ineligible to vote in general elections
– is illegitimate. It takes the nominating decision away from the
party's long-time activists and places it in the hands of folks whose
commitment to the party is weak and fleeting. Those who toil for the
party in the unglamorous periods between elections should be
rewarded with making the nomination decision. The difficulty with
this position is that we know, from the data regarding the parties'
activist cores and from the interelection-period membership numbers
reported in Chapter 2, that this approach would mean the nominating
electorate would be almost exclusively of European origin with few
new Canadians voting.

It is also worth noting that this argument is raised almost exclusively in the cases of mobilization of ethnic minorities and not during
the typical membership increases experienced in most parties during

competitive nomination contests. The reaction is harsher when the new recruits look and speak differently from the party's core group. Some party activists, particularly in the Canadian Alliance, have called for a citizenship requirement for participation in nomination contests. For instance, Alliance MP Rob Anders complained bitterly about ethnic mobilization in some of the party's nomination contests for the 2000 election, saying, "You have a lot of people who either can't read the language, can't speak the language, come to the voting process and are basically instructed by others how to vote" (Harrington 2000).

Others defend these membership recruitment drives as a way of socializing new Canadians into the political process and into the parties. They argue that it is healthy for new immigrant groups to strengthen their attachment to Canadian public life by participating in political events, and that nomination contests provide this opportunity. The difficulty with this view is that it is difficult to discern what lasting benefit many of these voters get from voting in a nomination contest. Many of them seem to be recruited to participate for the sole purpose of supporting a particular candidate. Thus, it is not the case that they are educating themselves about the candidates and the important issues and casting a deliberative ballot, although in this respect they act like many nomination voters. As the Alliance MP Anders suggested, many are supporting a candidate they know little about but have been instructed to vote for by a respected leader in their community. The data reported in Chapter 2 also illustrate that virtually none of these new members from ethnic and visible minority groups remain in the parties beyond the nomination campaigns. Just before the 2000 campaign there were very few non-European Canadians in any of the parties; nearly all of those who had been mobilized to support candidates in the 1997 election had apparently fallen from the membership rolls.

Perhaps the most compelling argument on the positive side of the ledger is the possibility that these recruitment efforts offer increased political clout to ethnic and visible minority communities. Because they have repeatedly displayed an ability to mobilize large numbers of voters, the support of opinion leaders in these communities is vigorously sought after. This provides an opportunity for community leaders to discuss issues of particular concern in their communities with prospective candidates and to assess the candidates' sensitivity to them. Better yet, in terms of improving representation, in recent elections at both the provincial and federal levels, members of minority groups have mobilized to support nomination candidates from their own communities. The open nature of the process allows candidates from different backgrounds than those of the typical party elite to successfully challenge for nominations. Thus, it seems that participation in nomination contests offers little in terms of political socialization for most of the individuals recruited to them, but that the open nature of the contests provides minority communities with a potentially significant political voice.

Representativeness of Nominated Candidates

Attention often focuses on the fact that members of legislative assemblies in Canada are not representative of Canadian society at large. Much is made of the underrepresentation of women and visible minorities in these institutions. But less attention is paid to the inclusiveness of the candidate nomination process that produces the pool from which legislators are chosen. As long as women and visible minorities are significantly underrepresented among nominated candidates, they are sure to be underrepresented in the parties' legislative caucuses. (Two useful studies of women's experiences in nomination contests are Erickson 1991 and 1993.)

Generally speaking, formal barriers to becoming a candidate for party nomination are few. Nomination is usually open to all Canadian citizens over the age of eighteen. Candidates are often not required to live in the riding they seek to represent, and there is typically no fee to enter a nomination contest. Some parties conduct background checks aimed at eliminating those with serious criminal records and the like, and some, such as the Alliance, require candidates to pledge their agreement with the party's general ideology.

Nonetheless, in the 2000 federal election, more than 80 percent of candidates nominated by the major parties were male, and fewer than 10 percent were a visible minority. Given these numbers it is not surprising that women continue to comprise only 20 percent of those elected to the House of Commons and visible minorities a paltry 5 percent (compared to more than 12 percent of the Canadian population).

The numbers of women and visible minority candidates nominated by the different parties vary dramatically. For example, as shown in Table 4.1, the NDP nominated three times more women in the 2000 federal election than did the Alliance. Information on the number of visible minorities nominated is somewhat sketchier. We are reliant on the parties for this information and they do not all collect it (nor do they all define the term the same way). Nonetheless, from news reports during the 2000 election campaign we can estimate that less than 8 percent of the candidates nominated by the major parties were visible minorities. The Bloc reported nominating six "ethnic minority" candidates and the Alliance twenty, while the Liberals reported twenty-five "visible minority" candidates and the New Democrats twenty. No comparable numbers are available for the Conservatives.

The problem is not simply the outcomes of candidate nomination contests, but that few women and visible minorities enter them. Studies of both the 1988 and 1993 elections indicate that two-thirds of party associations had no women candidates for their local nomination

Table 4.1

Percentage of nominated candidates who are female

	1993 (%)	1997 (%)	2000 (%)
Bloc Québécois	13	21	23
Canadian Alliance/Reform	11	10	10
Liberals	22	28	22
New Democrats	38	36	31
Progressive Conservatives	23	19	13

and that most of the women competing were challenged by a male opponent (Carty and Erickson 1991, 348; Cross 1996b, 178). Almost nine in ten associations had no visible minority candidates for their nomination in the 1993 election (Cross 1996b, 181). The norm that incumbents are not challenged is a factor in the low number of associations with female and visible minority nomination candidates, as the vast majority of incumbents are white men. However, even in associations without an incumbent, women and visible minorities are significantly less likely than white men to seek a party nomination.

Women seem to compete as well as men when they enter nomination campaigns. The last election for which we have data on the number of women contesting nomination is 1993. In this election, local associations with a woman seeking the nomination actually nominated a female candidate most of the time. This finding is consistent with what Carty and Erickson conclude about the 1988 election. They report that women were nominated in 61 percent of the contests they entered and conclude, "The problem, it seems, is that women do not contest candidacies to the same extent as men" (Carty and Erickson 1991, 147).

The parties take very different approaches to attracting candidates from underrepresented groups. Most of the parties establish local candidate recruitment committees in advance of each election, and some encourage these committees to seek out well-qualified female and visible minority candidates. Erickson (1991) suggests that these committees are important in encouraging more women to run. She found that when a local association had a search committee, there was a 60 percent increase in the likelihood of there being a woman candidate for the nomination. (Interestingly, the number of female Conservative candidates declined significantly after the party disbanded its women's commission in 1995.) Similarly, many suggest that one of the barriers visible minorities face is that personal networks within the parties at the local level are often important for identifying candidates and that members of minority groups are often not included within these networks. At the time of the 1993 election, the vast majority of local associations reported that a small core group organized most of the association's events. Six out of ten of these associations reported that there were no visible minorities within the core group.

Unsurprisingly, the New Democrats typically nominate more candidates from underrepresented groups than do the other parties. The federal NDP has adopted a comprehensive "nomination and affirmative action policy" that sets out detailed steps local and regional party associations must undertake to increase the representation of these groups in the party's parliamentary caucus. This document begins by establishing the following goals:

- A minimum of 60 percent of ridings where the NDP has a reasonable chance of winning shall have women running as NDP candidates for election.
- A minimum of 15 percent of ridings where the NDP has a reasonable chance of winning shall have NDP candidates for election who reflect the diversity of Canada and include representation of affirmative action groups.
- Ridings currently held by the NDP, where the incumbent is not seeking re-election, shall be given special attention to try to ensure that affirmative action candidates become NDP candidates for election (New Democratic Party 1997).

The party goes much further than just setting these objectives. Riding associations are required to establish candidate search committees and to actively solicit potential female and minority candidates. These efforts must include a series of pre-election workshops aimed at encouraging members of these underrepresented groups to stand for nomination. Local party associations without any affirmative action candidates for their nomination must satisfy party officials that substantial effort was made to recruit affirmative action candidates before the association's nominee is approved by the central party. Affirmative action candidates are also offered financial assistance. They are eligible for reimbursement of up to $500 for child care expenses incurred in seeking a nomination, $500 for travel costs in geographically large ridings, and an additional $500 for costs incurred in seeking nomination in ridings where the NDP incumbent is retiring. The party also allows these candidates to receipt three times as much funds as other candidates through the party for purposes of allowing their contributors to take advantage of the generous tax credit afforded to parties (the tax credit provision is discussed in Chapter 7).

It is noteworthy that the party provides special incentives to female and minority nomination candidates in ridings where it has retiring incumbents. Along with ridings where the party has incumbents seeking re-election, these are among the ridings where it has the best chance of winning. These provisions thus work to improve not only the chances of women and minority candidates being nominated but also the chances of electing them to the legislature (38 percent of federal NDP members elected in 2000 were women). Other parties have been criticized for increasing their overall number of women and minority candidates by disproportionately nominating these candidates in ridings the party has no hope of winning.

The other parties take less extensive steps to encourage female candidates. Jean Chrétien set a target of 25 percent of Liberal candidates being women in the elections of 1997 and 2000. To achieve this goal, the party's provincial campaign chairs sometimes pressured riding associations with open nominations to recruit women and, as discussed above, Chrétien appointed some female candidates (and at least one visible minority). Activists in both the Conservative and Liberal parties have established funds to assist nominated women candidates with their campaign expenses; however, unlike the NDP, neither of these parties provide funding to female candidates before they are nominated. The Alliance, on the other hand, takes the position that all potential candidates should be treated equally with no groups receiving preferential treatment. As with its refusal to create constituent categories of members (e.g., women, youth, minorities), the party takes no formal steps to encourage the participation of women or visible minorities as candidates for local nominations. Party rules do require local associations to establish a candidate search committee well before each election. These committees are charged simply with finding the best available nominee. The committee mandate makes no reference to encouraging the candidacy of women or others from underrepresented groups.

The costs of competing in nomination campaigns are often pointed to as a significant factor in discouraging female and minority candidacies. The 1991 Royal Commission on Electoral Reform and Party Financing (1:107) reported that "during our hearings at the symposium on women in federal politics and in surveys, women identified cost as the most formidable obstacle to nomination," and "women appear to lack the professional or social contacts needed to build financially competitive campaign organizations." Other underrepresented groups also report that costs are a key barrier to seeking nominations. For example, a representative of the Canadian Association of the Deaf said, of seeking a party nomination, "For the average able-bodied person, it is a very expensive gamble to undertake. For a deaf or otherly-disabled person it is quite frankly prohibitive" (Royal Commission 1991, 1:96). The commission recommended that parties establish a nomination spending limit, and that financial incentives be available to assist with child-care costs.

The parties have responded variously to these concerns. The Conservatives and the Alliance have declined to set a limit on the amount nomination candidates can spend, while the New Democrats and Liberals have set dramatically different limits. The NDP spending limit is $5,000, and the Liberal limit in the 2000 election was 50 percent of the permitted spending by the party's nominated candidate in the last general election. This amount varies by riding, but the formula generally allowed Liberal nomination candidates to spend approximately $35,000. However, it is widely believed that the vast majority of nomination campaigns spend considerably less than this amount.

The parties have also taken different approaches to enforcement of these self-imposed limits, ranging from automatic loss of candidacy for anyone found in violation (NDP) to vesting complete enforcement discretion with their campaign chairs and requiring only that they act in the best interests of the party (Liberal). Of course, a party's campaign co-chairs would seem unlikely ever to find it in the best interest of the party to publicly reprimand (and perhaps remove) a nominated candidate during the course of an election campaign because of a spending impropriety. It is important to reiterate that these rules were made, changed, and enforced at the parties' sole discretion. As discussed in Chapter 7, campaign finance legislation passed by Parliament in 2003 includes, for the first time ever, statutory limits on spending in nomination contests. This legislation caps spending at 20 percent of that allowed in a general election, or approximately $15,000. Many women's groups applauded the new limit, saying it would make it easier for women to compete for the most highly sought-after nominations.

Broadening Involvement in Candidate Nomination

Through candidate nomination the political parties exercise significant influence over who represents Canadians in their legislatures. Considering the increased regionalization of the Canadian party system, in many parts of the country the nomination contest is more significant than the general election. For example, consider federal politics in Ontario. In the elections of 1993, 1997, and 2000, Liberal candidates won in 99 percent of the province's constituencies. In effect, the choice of an MP was made in Liberal nomination contests. Similarly, Reform and then Alliance candidates swept many Western constituencies with large pluralities. As for a Liberal in Ontario, the major obstacle for a would-be Reform MP from one of these ridings was the nomination contest rather than the general election.

Given the importance of these contests, from a participatory perspective it is discouraging that such a high percentage of them are uncontested and that so few people routinely vote in them. The obstacles to participation in terms of accessibility of the process are significant enough to deter many partisans from participating. One wonders why payment of a party membership fee, travel to a single location in a riding, and sitting through a two- or three-hour meeting should be required of those wanting a say in who their party's nominee will be. It is difficult to make a compelling case as to why participation in these contests should be substantially more burdensome than voting in a general election. Surely a more accessible process would encourage more Canadians to participate.

Nomination contests are highly instrumental in determining the numbers of women and visible minorities elected to our legislatures. When parties nominate few representatives of these groups, they perpetuate their underrepresentation. There is no evidence that voters are less likely to support a female or minority candidate either in a nomination contest or in a general election. In fact, when women seek party nominations they succeed in numbers equal to men, and when women are nominated in competitive ridings, they are elected at rates similar to men. Parties are the gatekeepers to elective office. Their challenge is to encourage more members of underrepresented groups to compete for nominations, and to create processes that are welcoming to them and maximize their chances for success.

The parties' recruitment function is not limited to local candidates. Leadership selection is also a central responsibility of the parties. As described in the next chapter, many of the issues relating to participation, inclusiveness, and responsiveness in nomination contests also apply to leadership selection.

Chapter 4

Candidate Selection

Strengths

- The selection of candidates is generally left to the discretion of local partisans.
- Recruitment drives in contested candidate nomination contests routinely bring in hundreds of new voters.
- Most of the parties are taking affirmative steps to increase the numbers of women and visible minority candidates. The New Democrats are leading the way in these efforts.

Weaknesses

- Central party officials, particularly in the Liberal Party, are increasingly interfering with the ability of local associations to nominate the candidate of their choice.
- A very small percentage of general election voters participate in candidate nomination contests.
- Many nomination contests, particularly those with incumbents seeking renomination, are uncontested.
- Discussion of public policy is generally discouraged during nomination contests.
- Parties continue to nominate few women and visible minority candidates.

5 SELECTION OF PARTY LEADERS

Leadership selection is one of the most important and consequential functions of Canada's political parties. Leaders dominate election campaigns, exercise significant influence over the parties' parliamentary agendas, and fill important parliamentary positions including those of premier and prime minister. Notwithstanding the central importance of party leaders in Canadian politics and government, voters are never given the opportunity to pass judgment on who should fill these positions. This power is reserved for party members.

Given the importance of party leaders, it is not surprising that party activists have routinely sought to open up the selection process to more grassroots participation and to make the process both more inclusive and responsive. From selection by the governor general, to election by the parliamentary caucus, to delegate conventions, and finally to every-member votes, the history of party leadership selection in Canada is one of continual pressure for an expanded electorate, with greater rank-and-file participation.

In comparison with other parliamentary democracies, Canada has been at the forefront in devising selection methods that include an ever growing number of voters in the leadership decision. Nevertheless, only a fraction of any party's partisans participate in the leadership choice. The obstacles to participation imposed by the parties are higher than those to voting in general elections organized by the state. Parties have successfully argued that selecting a leader is an internal matter, and thus participation should be limited to their members and organized in whatever fashion they deem appropriate. This chapter considers whether this position is defensible given the consequential nature of leadership selection beyond the interests of the political parties, the substantial barriers to participation the parties continue to impose, and the relatively few Canadians who participate in these votes.

Consideration is also given to the challenges parties face in fashioning a selection process that encourages grassroots partisans to participate while maintaining the opportunity for collective decision making. Delegate conventions offer an ideal opportunity for party supporters from across the country to gather in a single location and jointly consider the leadership choice. Where they fall short is in providing a meaningful role for the vast majority of party partisans who are not attending the convention. Alternatively, direct election of leaders by the party membership allows widespread participation but little or no opportunity for collective deliberation. Members of most parties cannot gather at a common place and time to consider the leadership choice, because of Canada's size and geography. The federal Conservatives and Liberals have adopted methods that combine the participatory advantages of every-member votes with the collective decision making of the delegate convention. This hybrid method appears well suited to parties charged with the task of building accommodative bridges across the deep linguistic and regional cleavages that so often divide Canadians.

The chapter concludes with the question of leadership removal. Democratic concerns about how leaders are chosen lose much of their urgency if party members have no way to remove an unwanted leader. The parties have had formal methods of leadership review for more than three decades. During this time there have been many struggles between leaders wanting to hold on to their jobs and supporters of would-be leaders looking to push the incumbent out. The greatest contemporary challenges surrounding leadership review concern the role of the parliamentary caucus, and determining which party body has a legitimate right to challenge, and perhaps end, the term of a leader selected through a vote of the entire party membership. (Consideration of the financing of leadership campaigns is reserved for Chapter 7.)

The Evolution of Leadership Selection

For the first fifty years following Confederation, Canadian political parties followed the British model of the time, which left leadership selection solely to the discretion of those members of the party elected to the legislature. The process was not even always inclusive of all members of the legislative caucus. In the case of the governing party, the agreement of the governor general was usually required, and in every case elites among the caucus had more influence than did rank-and-file members. Party activists outside of the legislature played no direct role in the selection of leaders during this period. Political parties had little or no formal organization outside of Parliament and, at least in the case of leadership selection, the parliamentary caucus was the party.

The first significant opening up of the process occurred in 1919 when the Liberals became the first national party to select their leader at a convention of party elites. They were choosing a successor to Wilfrid Laurier, who had been leader for more than thirty years. Laurier's death had come on the heels of the Liberals' drubbing in the election of 1917. The election campaign of that year had revolved around the issue of conscription during the First World War. Laurier's opposition to conscription (a position widely supported in French-speaking Canada and opposed elsewhere) had resulted in a Liberal caucus dominated by Québécois. Realizing the need to expand their electoral support into English Canada, the party's elite supported the selection of an English-speaking Protestant leader. The problem was that there were no suitable candidates within the caucus, three-quarters of whom were Québécois. By chance, the party had already issued a preliminary call for a policy and planning convention for later that year. Without a suitable candidate in caucus, and faced with the difficulty of a

Quebec-dominated caucus identifying and choosing an appropriate non-Quebecer from outside the caucus, the party's leadership decided to let the convention decide.

This decision was portrayed as favouring a more democratic and representative selection process. William Lyon Mackenzie King, who was not a member of the parliamentary caucus, was chosen leader in a hotly contested race with three other candidates that was decided on a third ballot by the almost 2,000 convention delegates. While the convention did include a good number of central party elites as delegates, there were also representatives from party constituency groups from across the country. In 1927 the federal Conservative Party largely ended the practice of selecting leaders by a vote of caucus members when it held a convention to choose a successor to Arthur Meighen. (For a full discussion of this history, see Courtney 1973.)

It is important to note that a wider movement in support of more participatory and representative politics existed at the time. This period was marked by the emergence of the populist farmers' parties in western Canada and Ontario. Supporters of these parties believed the Liberals and Conservatives to be elite driven and unresponsive to the concerns of ordinary Canadians. The farmers' parties formed governments in several provinces, and, as the Progressive Party, elected the second-largest number of MPs in the federal election of 1921. It is impossible to quantify the influence of this phenomenon on the internal workings of the Conservative and Liberal parties. However, the changes in leadership selection ushered in by the old-line parties were certainly to some extent a reaction to the resonance the new parties were finding among voters with their portrayal of the traditional parties as elite driven and undemocratic.

For the next several decades, party leadership selection took place at what might best be described as semi-open, moderately competitive conventions. The two Liberal conventions of 1948 and 1958 are illustrative. The 1948 convention was called to choose a successor to Mackenzie King. King let it be widely known that he preferred his justice minister, Louis St. Laurent, who was chosen from among three candidates with the support of two-thirds of the first-ballot voters. A decade later, it was no secret that St. Laurent wished to be succeeded by his external affairs minister, Lester Pearson. Pearson also faced two competitors and was chosen on the first ballot with close to 80 percent of the votes cast. Similarly, in the five Conservative conventions held between 1927 and 1956, three were decided on two ballots and the latter two on one. In 1948, George Drew won two-thirds of the first-ballot vote, and in 1956 John Diefenbaker won on the first ballot with 60 percent of the vote. By the mid-1960s it had been almost fifty years since the Liberals had held a competitive leadership contest and a quarter-century since the Conservatives had.

The conventions during this period ranged in size from about 1,200 to 1,700 delegates. While these delegates were certainly more diverse than the parties' parliamentary caucuses, they were still far from representative of the general population. Convention delegates were overwhelmingly male and from the middle and upper classes. Very few younger Canadians were found at these conventions. A large portion of delegate positions were reserved for what are called ex-officio delegates. These are people who come to their delegate status because of a position they hold in the party (a member of a legislative assembly, a past federal candidate, a member of the party's executive, and so forth). For example, in the Liberal convention of 1958, delegates were almost equally distributed between the ex-officio ranks and those chosen to represent constituency associations by the party's rank-and-file membership (Courtney 1995).

While the conventions of this era substantially broadened the franchise in party leadership selection, they were not the open, competitive, and representative affairs that party members were beginning to demand by the 1960s. There was substantial criticism among party activists that party decision making in general, including leadership selection, was too restrictive and not sufficiently inclusive of the parties' grassroots supporters. There were particular demands for more representation of women and youth. As in the earlier transition period, these demands for more participatory party democracy were part of a larger societal value shift toward greater inclusiveness in public life and skepticism about elite-dominated decision making. When the

Conservatives met in 1967 to choose a successor to Diefenbaker, and the Liberals in 1968 to choose a successor to Pearson, these conventions marked the beginning of the third era of party leadership selection.

Continuing the trend toward more participatory, inclusive, and responsive leadership selection, the convention processes in both of the major parties became dramatically more open. The most obvious change was in the number of delegates and competitive candidates. The Conservative and Liberal conventions of 1967 and 1968 each had approximately 2,300 delegates, in each case 1,000 more than their previous meeting. The contests were also considerably more open and competitive. There were eight serious contenders for the Liberal leadership and nine for the Conservative. Robert Stanfield was elected on the fifth ballot with 54 percent of the vote, and Pierre Trudeau won the Liberal contest on the fourth ballot with 51 percent support.

These trends continued through the conventions of the 1970s and 1980s. Joe Clark won the 1976 Conservative contest on the fourth ballot, defeating eleven candidates. In the party's 1983 contest, Brian Mulroney defeated seven candidates with a fourth-ballot victory. In the Liberal leadership race of 1984, which was contested by seven former and current cabinet ministers, John Turner won on the second ballot. The conventions also continued to grow in size. There were 3,000 delegates to the 1983 Conservative convention and 3,400 to the Liberals' gathering a year later (Courtney 1995).

The composition of convention delegations was also changing. The proportion of delegates chosen at the constituency level (as opposed to ex-officio delegates) continued to climb. The percentage of ex-officio delegates fell from 42 percent in the 1958 Liberal contest to 29 in the party's 1984 convention. On the Tory side, there was a similar drop from 46 percent in 1956 to 33 percent in 1983. While still not reaching numbers reflective of the general population, the number of women and youth delegates also increased dramatically. Close to 40 percent of delegates were women and one in four was under age twenty-four (Courtney 1995). Other representational imperatives found their way to the fore as the parties' rules set aside delegates for specific groups such as students and Aboriginals.

These post-1960 conventions were clearly more open, competitive, participatory, inclusive, and responsive to the parties' grassroots than were the leadership selection processes that preceded them. However, from a democratic perspective, they had a dark side. With the increase in the number of delegates chosen from the constituency level, the focus of competition in leadership campaigns shifted away from the convention to what has come to be known as "trench warfare" at the constituency level. Leadership candidates began to mobilize supporters to elect convention delegates supportive of their candidacies. This strategy led to an exponential increase in the cost of leadership campaigns and the mobilization of large groups of voters with little or no attachment to the party for purposes of packing delegate selection meetings. The number of candidates able to mount the type of lengthy, professional campaign required to be competitive declined, reducing the competitiveness of the contests. Overall, the importance of conventions as deliberative gatherings was reduced. A general perception also emerged that the representational imperatives had gone too far and were actually discriminating against party members not belonging to the targeted groups. As in 1919 and 1967, the existing method of party leadership selection, ushered in as a democratic reform, came to be seen as old-fashioned, elite controlled, and generally out of step with evolving democratic norms.

The last of the major parties' traditional leadership contests highlighted these concerns. When the Liberal Party met in Calgary in 1990, 4,500 delegates assembled, making it the largest meeting ever of its kind. There were, however, only two candidates with the slightest chance of winning. For the first time in more than three decades a major party convention was decided on the first ballot when Jean Chrétien easily outpolled his nearest rivals. The Conservatives attracted 3,500 delegates to their 1993 convention but again there were only two viable candidates, and Kim Campbell emerged victorious on the second ballot.

Potential candidates in these leadership races, such as former Liberal cabinet minister Lloyd Axworthy and Conservative cabinet minister Perrin Beatty, found that they could not raise the funds necessary to compete successfully. Chrétien spent in excess of $2.5 million, while Campbell topped the $3 million mark. The campaigns in both parties were marked by bitter constituency-level contests as forces loyal to the leading candidates worked to sign up supporters to pack local delegate selection meetings. Charges were raised that organizers were happy to bring in any warm body, regardless of whether a person had any allegiance to the party, could speak either of Canada's official languages, or, in a few cases, was sober. The only concern was that the new members vote for delegates supporting the organizers' preferred candidate.

The result of this organizational push was that conventions lost much of their drama and their importance as deliberative gatherings. A large number of delegates made up their mind on which candidate to support before attending the convention (in many cases, before seeking a delegate position) and the conventions came to be seen as expensive and extravagant celebrations where new leaders were crowned.

Direct Election

Largely in response to criticisms of the delegate convention and to evolving democratic norms, parties in the late 1980s and 1990s began selecting their leaders through a direct vote by the party membership. In this method, the members cast a ballot directly for their preferred leadership candidate (as opposed to voting for delegates to a convention), and the winner is determined by the preferences of the membership at large. In 1985 the Parti Québécois became the first major Canadian political party to select its leader through direct election. In the next decade provincial parties of nearly all political persuasions and from all regions of the country followed suit (Cross 1996a).

When parties decide to choose their leaders through direct election they inevitably argue that it is a more democratic process than the delegate convention. They base this argument primarily on three points: (1) direct elections are more accessible to grassroots members than are leadership conventions; (2) the participation of members in direct elections is more meaningful than participation in delegate selection meetings, as each member can cast an unmediated vote for his or her preferred leader; and (3) all voters are treated equally in that each is allowed only one vote.

As direct election became the method of choice at the provincial level, and was widely seen as more democratic than the old-style conventions, pressure mounted for the federal parties to abandon the delegate convention. The new method was first adopted by the Reform Party and the Bloc Québécois. The Bloc shares the social-democratic roots of its provincial partner, the Parti Québécois, and found it easy to follow in the PQ's footsteps in this regard. Reform was a champion of direct democracy and populism and thus also easily embraced direct election. After their electoral devastation of 1993, the Conservatives were looking for ways to revitalize the party and to recapture former supporters from the upstart Reform. As part of a series of initiatives aimed at "democratizing" the party, the Conservatives adopted direct leadership selection in 1995.

The federal Liberals have adopted a hybrid method that amounts to a combination of delegate convention and direct election merged into a single selection process, and the Conservatives, after using pure direct election only once (in 1998 to again select Joe Clark as their leader), have also moved to the hybrid model (described below). Both parties have struggled with fashioning a process that respects both the changing democratic norms that demand grassroots members have a direct vote in the leadership choice, and their preference as brokerage parties for collective decision-making processes. The evaluation of direct election that follows pays special attention to this challenge.

The New Democrats, largely concerned about reducing the influence of their organized labour supporters in the leadership choice, also resisted the movement to direct election. Nonetheless, in July 2002, in the wake of Alexa McDonough's resignation as leader, the NDP decided to elect her successor by a direct vote of the party's members.

METHODS OF DIRECT ELECTION

Because party leadership selections are essentially viewed in law as
private events of private organizations, for the most part they are not
publicly regulated. Parties are consequently free to establish any rules
and use any process they wish. Because each method of direct election
has different results in terms of participation rates, representativeness of the electorate, accessibility, and opportunities for deliberation,
it is useful to briefly consider these key variables of the types of
processes used. Direct elections have been conducted using various
voting methods, including telephone votes, mail-in ballots, one central
convention, regional voting sites, riding-based voting, and different
combinations of the above. For the first time ever in Canada, New
Democrats added Internet voting when they picked Jack Layton as
their new leader in January 2003. In addition to how votes are cast,
two other variables affect the democratic quality of the process: who
gets to vote, and the method of translating votes cast into the selection of a new leader.

Telephone voting has been used by several provincial parties and,
at the federal level, by the Canadian Alliance. In these contests, voters
are typically given a personal identification number (PIN) and a toll-
free telephone number. During a prescribed period of several hours on
voting day, members call the telephone number and enter their PIN
followed by additional numbers representing the candidate they wish
to vote for. In mail-in voting (used by the federal New Democrats, in
the second Alliance contest, and by several provincial parties), the parties send a ballot to all eligible members and voters have several days
to mail their completed ballot back to the party's headquarters.

At least one party, the PEI Conservatives, held a direct vote via a
gathering of all interested party members in the provincial capital.
This process was similar to an old-style convention except there was
no delegate selection preceding it and all party members were welcome to attend and vote for their preferred leadership candidate.
Regional voting sites have been used by provincial parties including

the New Brunswick Conservatives. This was similar to the process used by the PEI Conservatives, except that five regional voting centres were set up. Every party member was invited to drive to one of these five locations in the province during the prescribed hours on voting day and cast a ballot. Riding-based votes have been used at the federal level by the Liberals, Bloc, the Alliance, and the Conservatives, and by several provincial parties, including the two largest provincial contests, the Alberta Progressive Conservative (PC) Party and the Parti Québécois. These processes are the most similar to general election voting. Members simply show up at polling places run by the party in each riding and cast a paper ballot.

While parties have established different rules concerning who gets to vote, every contest limits voting to party members. Two additional limitations are often imposed: a voting fee, and a requirement that members belong to the party for a certain length of time before being eligible to participate. By invoking one or both of these principles, parties have ensured that the potential leadership selectorate was not the entire electorate but rather a subgroup of their memberships: those members willing and able to pay a voting fee, and those who belong to the party before a cut-off date.

Voting fees in leadership races are common. They typically range from $10 to $25, and are sometimes in addition to the costs of joining the party (also typically about $10). The type of voting procedure used influences the amount of the voting fee. Parties using telephone voting have generally charged voters more in order to off-load the costs of the necessary technology. Parties using less expensive methods have tended to charge a voting fee of about $10. Some parties, notably the Alberta Conservatives and the federal Alliance, charged voters no fee at all beyond a modest membership fee.

Parties have adopted widely varying rules regarding the length of time members must belong to the party before being eligible to vote. At one extreme is the Alberta PC Party. In its 1992 contest, it imposed no deadline whatsoever. Albertans were welcome to show up at party polling places located throughout the province, join the party on the spot for a fee of $5, and cast a ballot. The party even allowed voters to sign up on the day of the run-off vote, held one week after the first ballot. More typical are thirty-day cut-off provisions, though longer periods are not unknown. In their 1992 contest, the Ontario Liberals limited voting to members who had belonged to the party for at least ninety days, and for its 2003 contest the federal NDP imposed a forty-five-day cut-off.

The votes cast in a direct election are translated into the selection of a new leader by essentially three different methods. The most common method, used by many provincial parties and by both the Bloc and the Alliance at the federal level, is to simply count up the votes cast and declare elected the candidate with a majority of the votes. If no candidate receives a majority, consecutive ballots are held until a majority decision is reached. Several parties, including the Ontario and federal Conservatives, have used a more complicated process. In this method, each local constituency is awarded a hundred votes. These votes are awarded to leadership candidates proportionate to the share of votes received by each candidate from voters in that constituency. For example, ten voters cast ballots in a riding, with five supporting candidate X, three candidate Y, and two candidate Z; candidate X therefore receives fifty votes from that riding compared to thirty for Y and twenty for Z. All ridings cast a hundred votes regardless of how many party members actually cast a ballot. Each riding association thus has equal influence in the leadership choice at the expense of providing each party member with equal influence. The third method guarantees a certain degree of influence in the leadership choice to a particular class of members. This is the principle adopted by the federal New Democrats. Members of affiliated labour unions are guaranteed to have their votes weighted so that they equal 25 percent of the total votes cast, regardless of how many union members actually participate.

VOTER PARTICIPATION IN DIRECT ELECTIONS

In terms of the democratic criterion of participation, the first questions to be considered concern the numbers participating. How many voters participate in direct elections? What percentage of a party's members and of its voters participate? How do these numbers compare with participation rates in both delegate conventions and leadership selection contests in other Western democracies?

As illustrated in Table 5.1, the number of voters participating in direct leadership elections has varied dramatically. This table includes twenty-two direct election leadership contests: sixteen provincial contests and six federal ones. At the federal level, the number of voters has ranged from more than 130,000 in the 2003 Liberal contest to

Table 5.1

Direct election participation rates

	Voters	% of party members	% of party's voters in previous election
Federal governing party			
Liberal (2003)	132,750*	25	2.5
Federal opposition parties			
Bloc Québécois (1997)	50,418	45	3.6
Progressive Conservative (1998)	47,089	52	1.9
Canadian Alliance (2000)	120,557	59	3.7
Canadian Alliance (2002)	88,228	71	2.7
New Democratic (2003)	44,707	54	3.1
Provincial governing parties			
Parti Québécois (1985)	97,389	64	7.4
Alberta PC (1992)	78,251	75	17.8
Saskatchewan NDP (2000)	19,465	81	12.3
Ontario PC (2002)	44,118	41	2.2
Provincial opposition parties			
Ontario PC (1990)	15,850	48	1.7
BC Social Credit (1993)	14,833	33	4.2
Ontario Liberal (1992)	11,296	63	0.9
Alberta Liberal (1994)	11,004	28	2.8
Nova Scotia Liberal (1992)	6,999	42	2.9
BC Liberal (1993)	6,540	49	1.3
New Brunswick PC (1997)	3,803	75	1.8
Saskatchewan PC (1994)	3,298	36	4.5
BC Reform (1994)	2,376	58	1.6
Manitoba Liberal (1993)	1,938	24	1.6
BC Social Credit (1994)	1,871	5	0.5
PEI PC (1990)	887	44	3.5

* The party has not released official vote totals; this number was reported in the media. See, for example, "Martin wins 90% of delegates," *National Post*, 22 September 2003, A1.

fewer than 45,000 in the 2003 NDP contest. Participation levels appear to be influenced by a number of factors, including the type of process used and the competitive status of the party. Participation has been highest in the riding-based processes, possibly because this is the voting method Canadians are most familiar with. All three of the largest provincial contests used this method.

Participation rates are significantly lower in contests in which a substantial voting fee is charged. The highest turnout rates, in terms of both party members and all voters, were realized in the Alberta PC, Saskatchewan NDP, and Parti Québécois races, all of which charged only a modest membership fee and no additional voting tax. One Nova Scotia Liberal Party official involved in organizing one of the first direct elections to charge a voting fee had the following to say: "We only achieved suffrage on the part of those who could pay $25 or $45 respectively. The disadvantage is obvious. Those who cannot afford $25 or $45, or those to whom it does not appear to be a sufficient priority, will not participate. I regret the disincentive to those who lack the means to afford that fee to participate" (MacEwan 1993, 6).

Participation rates are also higher when parties hold power at the time of their leadership contest. Of the provincial cases studied, the Saskatchewan NDP, the PQ, and Ontario and Alberta Conservatives, all in government at the time of their contests, drew significantly more voters than did any of the contests held in opposition parties. Similarly, the percentage of party members participating has been highest in governing parties, reaching a peak of 81 percent in the 2000 Saskatchewan NDP race. The effect of this variable is well illustrated by the last two Ontario Conservative contests. In 1990 Mike Harris was chosen leader of the third-place Tories by 16,000 voters, compared with the 44,000 who participated twelve years later in the direct vote to select his successor Ernie Eves as premier. Similarly, the Alliance drew approximately one-third more voters to its 2000 leadership vote than to its 2002 contest. In 2000 the party was riding high in the polls, had significant momentum coming out of the United Alternative project, and was thought to be very much on the upswing. By the time of the 2002 contest, the party had fallen dramatically in public opinion polls and was mired in bitter internal struggle. This tendency is not surprising, as we expect voters to be more interested in contests choosing a premier or potential prime minister than the leader of a relatively weak opposition party.

While participation rates have been strongest in the four cases when a premier was selected, in every case only a tiny proportion of voters, and often a minority of party members, participated. The required membership fee and early cut-off dates dampen participation rates. The Alberta PC race benefited from having no membership cut-off date. In fact, turnout increased dramatically on the second ballot as supporters of Ralph Klein, who trailed on the first ballot, recruited a significant number of new members between the two votes. (For more on this contest, see Stewart 1997.)

Direct elections do allow more party members to cast a direct vote in the leadership contest than did the delegate convention process. The largest conventions allow 3,000 or 4,000 party members to cast ballots for their preferred candidate, compared with 100,000 or more in the large direct elections. With delegate conventions, most party members are relegated to participating in delegate selection meetings, allowing them at best an indirect and mediated vote in the selection process. It is difficult to know with any certainty how many party members traditionally participated in delegate selection meetings. The best estimates are that between 50,000 and 100,000 members participated in these meetings in the PC and Liberal contests in the 1980s and 1990s (Perlin 1991a; 1991b). These, of course, were contests in highly competitive, national parties. The best federal party comparisons are the Alliance race of 2000, though even this is imperfect as the party was organizationally weak east of Ontario, and the 2003 Liberal contest. The Alliance contest drew considerably more voters than earlier delegate selection meetings in parties with a more national scope, and the Liberals attracted more voters in 2003 than they are estimated to have drawn to their 1990 contest. The Progressive Conservative Party of 1998 was a mere shadow of its former self, yet its direct election that year drew participants in numbers similar to its earlier delegate selection meetings. In terms of sheer numbers participating, direct elections appear to compare favourably with delegate convention processes.

While the trend in leadership selection in Canada has been toward consistently greater and more widespread participation, it is an inescapable fact that only a fraction of any party's electoral supporters participate in these contests. And while Canada leads the way in comparison with other parliamentary democracies (some of whom, like Australia, still select party leaders through votes of the parliamentary caucuses), participation rates in US presidential primaries are dramatically higher. Unlike their Canadian counterparts, US contests are organized by the state, consistent with the rules governing general elections, and accordingly take place on fixed dates with voting locations and methods identical to general elections (with the exception of those few states still using the caucus method for primary elections). These contests have no requirement of formal party membership and no voting fees. While Canadians often enjoy criticizing low voter turnout rates in US general elections, US presidential and gubernatorial primaries enjoy substantially higher participation rates than do Canadian leadership selection contests. For example, the overall participation rate in the 2000 presidential primary contests was 18 percent of the voting-age population. For primaries held on or before Super Tuesday, when the outcome was still in doubt, turnout rates exceeded 20 percent. The only Canadian contest to even approach these numbers is the Alberta PC race, which at least in process came closest to resembling a US-style primary. In the Canadian case, the prerequisite of party membership, the imposition of a "poll tax," and the perception that these are internal party contests (subject to no public regulation) probably dampen participation rates.

Indeed, candidates sometimes use party rules governing membership recruitment to make it more difficult for nonmembers to join and participate in a leadership contest. A recent example of this is the 2003 leadership campaign of Liberal Paul Martin. Martin first sought the party leadership in 1990, losing on the first ballot to Jean Chrétien.

Martin's campaign team largely remained in place during the thirteen years of Chrétien's leadership. Martin supporters quietly toiled at the grassroots level taking control of riding, provincial, and national party associations. All the while they recruited new members to the party who supported Martin's leadership aspirations. With the approach of Chrétien's retirement and a consequent leadership contest, they moved quickly to make it significantly more difficult for other leadership candidates to recruit new members to the party. Convinced that the existing membership was largely supportive of Martin, his supporters changed the party's rules in several large provinces in an attempt essentially to freeze the membership a year or two before the leadership campaign and effectively ensure Martin's success.

While this tactic raises all sorts of fairness questions for the campaigns of Martin's would-be leadership challengers, from the perspective of a democratic audit the most disconcerting aspect is that party rules are being used to dampen public participation in the leadership contest. Canadians would not tolerate obstacles such as poll taxes, ninety-day cut-off periods for voting eligibility, and efforts by candidates to freeze the composition of the electorate more than a year prior to the vote in general election contests. Nor would the Charter of Rights and Freedoms probably allow such barriers to democratic participation. However, because leadership contests are widely considered the private business of parties, no one has yet raised a Charter challenge to these practices and it is uncertain whether one would be successful.

INCLUSIVENESS OF DIRECT ELECTION

In terms of inclusiveness, we are interested in the representativeness of the leadership electorate and in the participation rates of such traditionally underrepresented groups as women. One of the arguments advanced by proponents of direct election is that because the processes are more easily accessible than attendance at a leadership convention, members of groups underrepresented in conventions are more likely to participate. Unfortunately, no data are available on the sociodemographic characteristics of participants in any of the federal party direct elections held to date. However, thanks to survey work conducted by political scientists in several provinces, we do have sociodemographic data on voters in several provincial direct election contests that we can compare with similar data of earlier convention goers. The evidence is conflicting on whether direct election produces a more representative electorate.

Some studies comparing voters in a provincial party's direct election with voters in the party's past delegate conventions have found the direct election voters to be more representative on some socio-demographic characteristics. For example, studies of the Alberta PC and BC Liberal parties found a significant increase in the percentage of female voters in the direct elections (in the Alberta PC case there was a 50 percent increase, in the BC Liberal case a 25 percent rise) (Stewart 1997; Blake and Carty 1994). Youth were often over-represented in the last generation of conventions as parties allocated delegates to postsecondary campuses and riding-based youth associations. Data from contests in the Alberta PC and Nova Scotia Liberal direct votes show a decline of about two-thirds in the participation of youth and students. Similarly, participation of senior citizens, often underrepresented in conventions, increased dramatically in the direct elections held by these parties (Stewart 1997; Adamson et al. 1994). However, a study of a direct election and a leadership convention held by separate provincial parties in New Brunswick just six months apart found no evidence that process affected the participation rates of various groups. Voters in the October 1997 Conservative direct election were very similar on all these sociodemographic measures with delegates to the April 1998 Liberal convention (Cross 2002c).

One representational characteristic that is undoubtedly affected by the process used is regional representation. As described above, traditional leadership conventions in the Liberal and Conservative parties distributed delegates evenly among local constituency associations. With some slight variance resulting from the addition of ex-officio delegates, every constituency was entitled to the same number of delegates. Thus provinces and regions were represented at the convention roughly proportionately to their populations. (The New Democrats

94

never accepted this principle; instead of distributing delegates evenly across the country they rewarded areas of strength, most noticeably the western provinces, with more delegates at the expense of regions where the party was electorally weak – Quebec and Atlantic Canada.) Indeed, one of the important considerations influencing the federal Liberal and Conservative parties to adopt conventions in the first place was a need to compensate for regional imbalances in their parliamentary caucuses.

In a direct election there is no way to ensure an equitable number of voters in each region: the electorate is comprised of whichever party members choose to participate. Logic dictates, and experience shows, that the electorate will come disproportionately from areas where a party has strong electoral support. In federal contests, direct election electorates tend to be much more representative of the regional strengths of a party and the major leadership candidates. For example, as popular support for the Conservatives waned in Quebec, voters from this province made up only 10 percent of the 1998 PC leadership selectorate compared with 19 percent of the delegates to the party's 1993 leadership convention. Conversely, the Atlantic provinces, which more than any region have remained loyal to the party during its recent electoral difficulties, were home to 18 percent of the voters in the 1998 contest. This figure compares with 12 percent of the delegates to the party's 1993 convention and 9 percent of the Canadian electorate.

The regional imbalance is equally striking in the 2002 Alliance contest. All four of the Alliance's leadership candidates represented either British Columbia or Alberta ridings in the House of Commons. Most of the party's electoral support is found in these provinces, while it has never elected a member from east of the Ontario-Quebec border. As a result, six in ten voters were from either Alberta or British Columbia, while one in fifty was from Quebec. Table 5.2 compares the breakdown by region of delegates to recent conventions of the major federal parties, the two direct elections mentioned above, and the general electorate.

Some parties have modified the system of direct election they use to account for this regional imbalance. As described above, rather than

Table 5.2

Representation by region in leadership selectorate in various contests

	Direct elections			Conventions		
	Percentage of electorate	1998 PC	2002 CA	1989 NDP	1990 Liberal	1993 PC
British Columbia	12	11	20	21	13	12
Prairies	17	18	50	37	20	22
Ontario	36	43	27	34	36	35
Quebec	26	10	2	2	19	19
Atlantic	9	18	3	6	14	12

Note: The NDP did not release regional results for its 2003 contest.
Sources: Convention numbers from Courtney 1995, 336; PC 1998 numbers from Stewart and Carty 2002, 61.

simply counting up the votes and declaring the candidate with a majority to be elected, they maintain the convention principle of regional balance by assigning each constituency 100 votes. Of course, this comes at the expense of the one member, one vote principle that is one of the legitimating forces for adoption of direct election. This point is well made in an article on the 1998 federal Conservative contest by David Stewart and Kenneth Carty (2002) that illustrates the dramatic difference in weight given to voters in different ridings. In the Ontario riding of Kingston and the Islands 1,300 people voted, compared with eight in the Quebec riding of Bellechasse-Etchemins-Montmagny-L'Islet. Because each riding was entitled to 100 votes, the votes in Kingston, once converted to a total of 100, were each worth 0.13, while each vote in Bellechasse counted for 12.5 votes. Each Bellechasse voter had ninety-six times greater influence in the outcome of the race than did each Kingston voter. Thus voters in areas where the party is weak have greater influence in the leadership decision than those in areas of strength. It is, however, incorrect to suggest that this situation did not exist in the convention era – it did. Whenever constituency associations are allocated the same number of delegates regardless of how many party members there are in the riding, activists in areas where the party is weakest have the greatest influence in the leadership choice.

Direct Election and Responsiveness

While direct elections clearly allow more party members to cast an unmediated vote for their preferred leader than do delegate conventions, other aspects of the democratic experience need to be considered. These include the effectiveness of the participation, the types of information available to leadership voters, the commitment of voters to the party, and the opportunity for voters to engage in collective decision making. Essentially, these concerns relate to the responsiveness of the process to the informed preferences of the party's supporters.

Because relatively few party members actually attend leadership conventions and the only opportunity for mass participation is in delegate selection meetings, it makes sense to compare voting in a direct election with voting for convention delegates. Voting in delegate selection contests is at best an indirect expression of support for a leadership candidate. There is evidence suggesting that even during the period of "trench warfare," when leadership candidates spent large amounts of time and money in efforts to have their delegate candidates elected, a majority of local delegate selection contests were not determined by preferences for particular leadership candidates. In a survey conducted subsequent to the 1990 and 1993 leadership conventions held by the federal Liberals and PCs, constituency association presidents were asked what they thought was the most consequential factor in determining which delegate candidates were chosen to attend the recent leadership convention. As shown in Table 5.3, half of local association presidents said the most important factor was how active the delegate candidates had been in local party affairs, while under one-third thought declared support for a particular leadership candidate to be the most important factor.

The traditional convention process also offers no guarantees that those delegates chosen because of their commitment to a particular candidate will actually vote for that candidate at the convention. Delegates are not bound by any prior commitments and all voting is conducted by secret ballot. Decisions about whom to support on subsequent ballots, when a preferred candidate may have been eliminated, are fully

Table 5.3

Most important factor in determining selection of delegate candidates

	Liberals (%)	Conservatives (%)
Length of time delegate candidate has been a party member	6	5
Declared support for a leadership candidate	33	23
Number of new party members signed up to support delegate candidate	14	19
How active the delegate candidate has been in party affairs	46	54
Number	(132)	(108)

Source: Mail survey of riding association presidents, 1994.

within the delegate's discretion. In these processes, the relationship between the party activists' participation in a delegate selection meeting and the ultimate choice of the party leader is tenuous at best. Direct elections fare much better on this count, as participants vote directly for their preferred leadership candidate.

A criticism of direct elections has been that voters in these contests have less information available to them in making their decision, and are dependent upon the media for most of the information they do have. When the electorate expands to tens of thousands of voters it becomes impossible for leadership candidates to meet them all personally. In the contests with the largest electorates it is also very costly for candidates to communicate with all voters by mail or telephone. And in those contests allowing voters to sign up as members (and thus become eligible to vote) seven days or less before the contest, candidates do not even have a complete list of the electorate in time to contact voters.

The 1992 Alberta Conservative contest, which selected Ralph Klein as premier, provides evidence to support the proposition that direct election voters are less likely to have personal contact with candidates and their supporters and instead are more dependent on the media. In this contest, only 30 percent of the electorate had met any of the candidates, 20 percent had attended an all-candidates forum, and fewer than half were contacted by a candidate. This contrasts with the party's 1985 convention, where most of the delegates had personally met at least one of the candidates (60 percent had met the winning candidate), more than half had been personally contacted by the weakest candidate in the race, and 60 percent had attended an all-candidates forum (Stewart 1997).

The large electorate in the Alberta Conservative race and the absence of a membership cut-off date reduced the candidates' ability to contact voters. In the New Brunswick leadership races discussed above, which involved an earlier membership cut-off date and substantially fewer voters, there was no significant difference in the voter contact rates in the direct election and the delegate convention. Liberal convention delegates were slightly more likely to have attended a candidate debate (three-quarters had done so, but so had two-thirds of voters in the Conservatives' direct election). In both parties, more than 80 percent of voters were contacted by candidates or their supporters before the vote (Cross 2002c, 46). However, at least in terms of size of the electorate, federal party direct elections are more similar to the Alberta PC case, and accordingly there is legitimate concern regarding the source of voter information in direct elections. More research is needed into this question. (Of course, most voters in general elections are also dependent on the media for information regarding the parties and their leaders.)

Another criticism of direct election is that the leadership decision is turned over to those who are not strongly committed to the party. The argument is that direct election contests are more permeable and more likely to attract voters who are not really committed partisans. The underlying assumption here is that long-term, committed party members make better decisions than do leadership voters with little or no activist experience and less commitment to the party. This argument was raised by supporters of Joe Clark during the 1998 Conservative contest. They contended that Clark's second-ballot opponent David Orchard, and his supporters, were not really Conservatives but were using the party to advance their own political agenda. Clark went so far as to call Orchard's supporters "tourists" to the Progressive Conservative Party. While it is true that many Orchard supporters were new to the party in 1998, many of them have since continued their involvement in Conservative party politics. Orchard won approximately one-quarter of the delegate votes at the party's 2003 leadership convention. Nonetheless, at the time of the 1998 leadership vote these newly recruited members had less history with the party than convention delegates would have had.

The New Brunswick cases provide further evidence of this point. Delegates to the Liberal convention were more committed to their party than were voters in the Conservative direct election. Liberal delegates were more likely to have volunteered in some capacity for the party in the past, to have spent more time per month on party activity, and to indicate an intention to volunteer for the party in the coming election campaign (Cross 2002c, 46). Similar results are found in other studies of provincial contests.

While party members with a longer history in the party may be more committed to its long-term interests and have a greater capacity for making a wise leadership choice (though there is no evidence to support the latter), the question that remains is why the choice of a party leader should be limited to these voters. This question is more important given that victors in party leadership contests often automatically become prime minister or premier without facing the electorate, as was the case with recent prime ministers Paul Martin, Kim Campbell, and John Turner and recent premiers Camille Thériault (New Brunswick), Lorne Calvert (Saskatchewan), Ernie Eves (Ontario), Bernard Landry (Quebec), Ujjal Dosanjh (British Columbia), Ralph Klein (Alberta), and others. We do not restrict participation in general election campaigns to the most engaged and well informed, and it is not clear that there is a strong case to do so in party leadership elections. Furthermore, parties constantly need to attract new members. As illustrated in Chapter 2, none of the parties has an abundance of members, and leadership contests should be viewed as a vehicle for attracting new members into the party, providing them with a meaningful role in party decision making, and then keeping them engaged in party affairs.

The small size of the electorate in leadership conventions permits all those making the leadership choice to come together in one physical space. This opportunity allows delegates the possibility of engaging in collective decision making with one another. Delegates mingle in the same hotels and convention halls for several days and share opinions concerning the leadership candidates in both formal and informal settings. Delegates thus encounter the concerns of others from different regions of the country and from different socioeconomic backgrounds. Voters can then consider how their preferred candidate might fare as leader in other parts of the country. This is particularly important in Canada's Liberal and Conservative parties, given their accommodative traditions.

This phenomenon was an important factor in the outcome of the 1983 Conservative convention. In the weeks leading up to the convention, John Crosbie was gaining support across English Canada and closing in on the front-running Clark and Mulroney. At the convention, where a sizable number of the delegates were Québécois, Crosbie's inability to communicate in French became an issue. There is anecdotal evidence that a significant number of anglophones who viewed Crosbie favourably ultimately decided not to support him because the reaction of Quebec delegates to Crosbie's candidacy, made clear at the convention, gave them doubts about his ability to lead a brokerage party. In particular, they were concerned that he could not win the substantial support in Quebec necessary to form a majority government. John Courtney (1995, 278) suggests that for 45 percent of the delegates to this convention, a candidate's perceived responsiveness to regional interests was very influential in their choice of whom to support. It is less likely that this sentiment would have had an important effect had the voters in the contest not physically gathered together and had the opportunity to share their views with one another.

Direct elections are much more atomistic than conventions. This is particularly true of telephone, mail, and Internet ballots that allow members to cast a vote without ever leaving home or perhaps even talking to another party member. In a country built on a tradition of parties seeking accommodative bridges across deep linguistic and regional divides, this is cause for concern. In considering whether to abandon the delegate convention in favour of direct election, the federal Liberals were deeply torn between a desire to maintain the collective and deliberative opportunities provided by the convention and the attractiveness of the more participatory and inclusive opportunities of direct elections. In the end the party chose Paul Martin as leader using a hybrid system intended to preserve the best of the convention while introducing the opportunity for direct, proportionate participation by all party members. The federal Conservatives also adopted a hybrid system and used it for the first time in selecting Peter MacKay as leader in 2003.

The hybrid process maintains the primary benefit of the direct vote in that all party members are given the opportunity to vote directly for the leadership candidate of their choice. The result of this vote determines, on a proportionate basis, how many delegates pledged to each leadership candidate are selected from each riding. Members also cast a separate ballot to select the actual delegates from among lists of delegate candidates committed to particular leadership hopefuls. Delegates are then required to vote in accordance with the results of the local members' vote on the first convention ballot. On any subsequent ballots they are free to vote as they please. In many ways this parallels the US presidential primary process, which couples direct votes with delegate conventions.

An example may help illustrate how this process generally works. Assume each riding is allowed to send eight delegates to the convention. All of the members in a riding gather and cast a ballot for their favoured leadership candidate. Candidate X receives 50 percent of the vote, Y receives 25 percent, and Z 25 percent. Candidate X is therefore entitled to four of the eight delegates from the riding while Y and Z each receive two. The identity of the actual delegates is determined by a separate (but simultaneous) ballot. Supporters of X vote for up to eight delegates from a list of candidates who have pledged themselves to voting for X on the first ballot, and Y and Z supporters do likewise for their candidates' delegates. Given the results of the leadership ballot in our hypothetical riding, the four delegate candidates pledging to support X with the most votes win delegate spots, as do the top two Y and Z delegate candidates.

This hybrid selection process has five benefits:

1 Party members cast a direct vote for leader, not solely for a delegate candidate.
2 Delegates are chosen on a proportionate basis reflecting the members' leadership preference.
3 Delegates are bound to follow the members' wishes on the first ballot.
4 Delegates are free to engage in collective decision making at the convention on any subsequent ballots.
5 Ridings are afforded an equal number of delegates ensuring equitable regional representation at the convention.

While the hybrid method brings together many of the best features of the traditional delegate convention and direct election, the methods used by the federal Conservatives and Liberals maintain some of the impediments to participation associated with the older-style conventions. For example, only fee-paying members are eligible to participate, voting takes place at only one location in most ridings, and membership cut-off dates remain in effect. In the 2003 Liberal contest, the actual selection of the leader occurred in November, but the cut-off date for interested voters to join the party in order to be eligible to vote in the contest was 20 June – five months before the leadership convention and three months prior to the selection of delegates.

Leadership Review

The question of leadership selection loses much of its importance if leaders can be replaced only when they either die or voluntarily retire. In order for the party membership to control the selection of a leader, it must also be able to remove an unpopular one. The history of leadership review in Canada is both recent and colourful.

For the first hundred years after Confederation, there was no for-mal mechanism in place for members of a party to challenge a sitting leader. Leaders were replaced only upon their retirement or their death. This changed in the mid-1960s when both the Liberals and Con-servatives adopted formal procedures for regular reviews of their lead-ers by their membership in convention. Leaders now have their tenure in office renewed by a periodic vote of delegates at party conventions. Leaders have many tools available to them in these contests, and no Canadian leader has ever actually lost a leadership review vote. Never-theless, relatively weak votes of support have caused both federal and provincial leaders to resign.

The classic example of this is the case of federal Conservative leader Joe Clark. After leading his party to victory in the 1979 general election after five consecutive defeats, Clark was widely criticized for his government's quick demise and subsequent defeat in the general election of 1980. Clark faced substantial opposition to his continuing as party leader, and on review votes in 1981 and 1983 he received the support of two-thirds of convention delegates. Though the party's con-stitution provided that the leader was removed only if a majority of convention delegates voted against his continued leadership, Clark resigned after the 1983 vote saying he could not continue in the face of such sizeable opposition. (He ran as a candidate in the subsequent leadership contest but was defeated by Brian Mulroney.)

The movement to leadership selection by a direct vote of the par-ties' members raises the difficult question of who has the authority to replace a leader chosen by tens of thousands of party members. Essen-tially, the issue is whether a leader selected by a large number of party members can be removed from office by a vote of far fewer convention delegates. Embattled leaders have argued that their mandate comes from the entire membership and that they should be subject to removal only by a vote of the membership. In a formal sense, most par-ties have dealt with this issue by adopting constitutional provisions calling for a poll of party members before a leader can be removed. In practice, this has proven impossible. The time and cost involved in such processes are considerable. This means that when a leader has substantial opposition from within, he or she, and the party itself, are faced with a long period of turmoil before the membership can ratify (or not) his or her continued leadership. Parties suffer substantial costs from such long periods of what is inevitably public turmoil.

A related concern is the appropriate role of the parliamentary caucus in leadership removal. The caucus lost the right to select the leader a century ago but, in practice, maintains in most circumstances the ability to remove the leader. Though the parties' constitutions no longer give the caucus this authority, recent events suggest that leaders cannot continue for long without the support of their parliamentary party. The Alliance leader Stockwell Day faced a caucus revolt in the aftermath of the party's disappointing showing in the 2000 election. A dozen Alliance members left the party's caucus amidst calls for Day's resignation. For several months Day resisted, arguing that his leadership could only be challenged by a vote of the membership, scheduled for the following year. The public feuding within the party resulted in a sharp decline in the party's position in public opinion polls and in its ability to raise funds. After months of intense party division, Day announced his resignation as party leader well before the scheduled date for review by the membership. The only conclusion is that Day was forced from the leadership (a position he won in what was at the time the most participatory leadership election ever held in Canada) because he no longer maintained the confidence of his parliamentary caucus.

Liberal prime minister Jean Chrétien similarly faced substantial opposition both from within the party's caucus and, allegedly, from the wider membership. By the spring of 2002, many caucus supporters of Chrétien's would-be successor, Paul Martin, were publicly and privately calling on the prime minister to resign. For months, like Day, Chrétien maintained that his leadership could be challenged only by a partywide vote scheduled for the following winter. However, as dissension within the caucus became increasingly public and bitter, Chrétien announced his intention to resign five months before the scheduled membership vote, which was subsequently cancelled (even though his resignation would not take effect for another sixteen months).

These two examples demonstrate that party leaders cannot continue in their position for long once they lose the support of their parliamentary colleagues. While the parties' rules might provide for a more participatory process of leadership review, in fact the principal task of the leader is to lead the parliamentary party. Once the parliamentary members no longer wish to be led by the incumbent, make this publicly known, and on occasion vote in Parliament in opposition to the leader's preference, his or her tenure is effectively over. While leaders may make a strong argument that a small, nonrepresentative body cannot legitimately remove them from an office won with the support of tens of thousands of party members, the political reality is that caucus holds the trump card in removing leaders. Caucus support may not be sufficient to keep an unpopular leader in his or her job (as was the case with Conservative leader John Diefenbaker in 1967) but the leadership cannot be maintained in the face of widespread caucus opposition.

Auditing Leadership Selection

The movement toward direct election of Canadian party leaders is a step in the right direction. The principal benefit of this method is that it allows the parties' grassroots members an opportunity to cast a consequential ballot directly for their preferred leadership candidate and not solely for slates of convention delegates. This method seems to have attracted more voters to the leadership selection process while providing them with more influence in the outcomes.

Nonetheless, it is peculiar that party leadership selection is considered a private event of the political parties. Selecting a leader (which often means selecting a premier or prime minister) is not like the choice of a party president or secretary. The latter are clearly internal party affairs. The importance of the leadership choice, however, goes far beyond the internal interests of the parties. In a democratic audit, one is left with the question of why the rules governing who gets to make this important decision should be left to the parties, especially when they have imposed obstacles such as poll taxes on participation and allowed individual candidates to essentially rig the rules in attempts to dampen participation rates.

The parliamentary form of Canadian general elections does not allow voters opportunity to express direct preferences for the offices of prime minister or premier. Instead voters choose from among the offered local candidates, and the leader of the party winning a plurality of these contests assumes the high office. This makes party leadership selection contests all the more consequential. Participation rates averaging well below 10 percent of a party's own partisans must be considered unacceptably low.

Modest public regulation, allowing any partisans (without the requirement of formal party membership) to participate in leadership contests, without requiring payment of a fee and in a manner that makes voting generally accessible, may serve to increase both participation rates and inclusiveness in the leadership selectorate. The suggestion of broadening participation in leadership selection (and local candidate nominations) beyond a party's fee-paying members is pursued more fully in the concluding chapter.

For parties seeking a leader with electoral appeal across Canada's deep regional cleavages, the hybrid method of leadership selection used by the federal Liberals and Conservatives is probably the best method. This method allows for widespread participation while preserving the opportunity for collective decision making. This probably explains why the two traditional brokerage parties have adopted it but their more regionally based competitors have not (particularly the Bloc and the Canadian Alliance). There is, however, no compelling reason why voting in the first stage of these contests need be restricted to fee-paying members who join prior to an early cut-off date and travel to a single location in each riding.

Since the advent of television, party leaders have become the dominant figures in election campaigns. The next chapter examines both local and national party campaign activity with special attention to the balance between local autonomy and centralized control exercised by the leader and his or her supporters.

Chapter 5

Leadership Selection

Strengths

- There has been a steady evolution toward more participatory and inclusive forms of leadership selection.

- Parties are allowed wide discretion in selecting leadership selection methods that reflect their particular democratic ethos.

- Federal Liberals and Conservatives have adopted methods that allow for direct, unmediated participation of their members while preserving the collective benefits of party leadership conventions.

Weaknesses

- Relatively few voters participate in leadership selection contests.

- Parties routinely impose substantial barriers to participation, including voting fees and membership cut-off dates.

- Parties are struggling with the question of who can fire a leader, particularly in those situations where the authority to select and to remove a leader lies with different groups within the party.

6   PARTIES AND ELECTION CAMPAIGNING

The primary activity of political parties, outside the legislatures, is the waging of election campaigns. Favoured by election laws that structure competition around the political parties, they are the dominant players in Canadian campaigns. As discussed in the earlier chapters, parties choose the individuals who contest elections – local candidates and party leaders. They also dominate the political debate that occurs during campaigns and the media's election coverage. This chapter examines the activities of parties during election campaigns, the role of both the parties' grassroots members and central operatives in campaign activities, and whether recent developments in campaigning add to the quality of democratic life in Canada.

Federal election campaigns have essentially two largely distinct loci of activity: national campaigns centred on the parties' leaders and the 301 local constituency campaigns. The national campaigns are dominated by long-time party insiders and political professionals, with essentially no role provided for grassroots activists. It is at the constituency level that regular Canadians have traditionally had the opportunity to participate in party campaign activity. Constituency campaigns are traditionally dominated by committed local volunteers and relatives, friends, and neighbours of the local candidates. Local volunteers are typically welcomed with open arms by candidates and their organizers desperate for enough person-power to carry out their planned campaign activities.

While local campaigns take place in all 301 ridings, and all of the parties, except the Bloc, run candidates in virtually all of them, the national campaigns pick and choose the ridings where they concentrate their efforts. The workings of Canada's first-past-the-post electoral system dictate that central parties focus on ridings where they have a chance of winning a plurality of the vote. The result is that while there are up to 301 local campaigns in most parties, the nature of the campaign effort, and the relationship between the local and central campaign office, differs substantially depending on a party's competitive position within a riding (for a good discussion of this, see Sayers 1998). While this chapter considers campaigning in all types of ridings, it focuses on the parties' efforts in ridings targeted as winnable. Even though these are a minority of the ridings in which many parties wage campaigns, they are the most consequential as they are the ones that might result in electoral victory.

As we shall see, in these key ridings parties are increasingly emphasizing the activities of their central campaigns at the expense of opportunities for meaningful participation by grassroots activists. Using ever more sophisticated methods of campaign communication, the parties are focusing on centralized communication strategies. In these ridings, volunteers are increasingly expected to implement standard strategies with little room for local exceptionalism. The central parties believe that vigorous local campaigns make only a marginal difference in election outcomes, but that the centralized activities of advertising and polling can make a significant difference. Aware that in a handful of the closest ridings the local effort may be determinative, the central operatives do not dismiss the activities of the local campaigns. Rather, in ridings where the outcome might be decided by a few hundred votes or less, the central campaign pays great attention to local campaign activity, in many cases to the point of taking over from the local activists.

This chapter also concludes that Canadian election campaigns are becoming increasingly regionalized and fragmented. Instead of there being one national political dialogue during the campaign, essentially a series of concurrent regional elections masquerades as a national campaign. Making use of advanced methods of public opinion polling and new communications technology, parties are also tailoring specific campaign messages to smaller and smaller groups of targeted voters. The result of these two phenomena is a shift away from the pan-Canadian campaigns that characterized electoral competition in the last half of the twentieth century.

The Local Campaign

Pre-election campaign planning at the local level revolves around fundraising and candidate recruitment. As discussed in Chapter 4, the central party plays an important role in this process. Regional and provincial campaign chairs spend considerable energy overseeing recruitment of preferred candidates and preventing the candidacies of less desirable ones. The bulk of central party attention in candidate recruitment is focused on ridings where the party believes it has a realistic chance of victory. A quality local candidate may offer a small boost to the party's electoral fortunes at the ballot box. An additional motivation for central party involvement is concern with the composition of the future parliamentary caucus. Central party figures, including the leader, pay close attention to candidate recruitment in ridings a party is likely to win, because of their interest in who will subsequently join the party's legislative team. As a consequence, in ridings where a party has little chance of electoral success (a majority of the ridings for most parties), the central party plays a minimal oversight role in the candidate nomination process.

Officials at central party offices point to interelection fundraising as one of the principal activities of local associations between election campaigns. In most parties, the central office expects riding associations to fully fund their local campaign efforts and to help support the national effort. Some parties prevent local associations from holding nomination meetings until they have raised a threshold amount of campaign funds. The flow of money within a party is typically upward from the local association to the provincial and national offices and not vice versa. The central parties often implement a withholding tax on all contributions submitted by local associations for a tax credit receipt. In order for donors to be eligible for the tax credit they require a receipt from the central party, which regularly withholds up to 25 percent of all contributions submitted by local associations. Similarly, some parties require that candidates agree, before their nomination papers are signed by the party leader, that if they are eligible for the retroactive 60 percent public funding (now given to candidates receiving at least 10 percent of the vote), all or a portion of these funds will be ceded to the central office. That fundraising is a central concern for local parties is evident in the findings of a survey of constituency associations conducted after the 1993 campaign. Local associations listed fundraising among the three most important election activities engaged in by their members (Cross 1996b, 264).

Volunteers

Once a candidate is nominated and fundraising efforts are under way, the local association's task is to attract sufficient volunteers to wage a visible and effective campaign. Local campaigns tend to focus on get-out-the-vote activities, which require considerable personnel. The 1993 campaign survey found that slightly more than six in ten associations were wholly dependent on volunteers; among the remaining associations, half had only one paid staff member. Interviews with party officials in the decade since then indicate that it is becoming somewhat more common for local campaign managers, and occasionally office managers, to be paid a modest salary. Central party staff help local associations identify experienced personnel to serve in these key roles. Some parties keep central "talent banks" to identify workers for key, targeted races across the country. The New Democrats regularly move campaign workers (often highly skilled union organizers) from one region to another so that their best, most experienced local staffers are deployed in their targeted ridings.

Nonetheless, the vast majority of local campaign workers are volunteers. The richest source of volunteers are friends, relatives, and
acquaintances of the local candidate. The 1993 survey found that six
in ten campaign volunteers participated because of a personal relationship with the candidate. In a recent federal campaign I visited the
office of a major party candidate in one of our largest cities. I was
greeted at the front desk by the candidate's mother, who was serving
as receptionist, then introduced to the candidate's father, who was
office manager, and the candidate's uncle, who was sitting at a nearby
table stuffing envelopes with campaign fliers. This is not uncommon:
local campaign teams reflect the candidates' personal networks. They
are personal supporters of the nominee who in many cases are not
committed partisans. One result is significant turnover in the local
volunteer corps as candidates change from election to election. This
affects the balance of power between the local and central organizations, as the local campaigns are often starting from scratch with each
new election.

The ability of a local candidate to attract large numbers of volunteers is especially important given that, as discussed in Chapter 2, the
active membership corps in most parties is very small between elections. The candidate must reinvigorate the local association, most
often by recruiting friends and neighbours (a process that starts with
the nomination meeting). Many local associations report difficulty in
finding enough volunteers. In the 1993 campaign, six in ten local associations reported an insufficient number of volunteers, and similar
findings were reported for the 1988 campaign (Cross 1996b; Carty
1991). Interviews with local campaign officials suggest this problem is
getting worse.

The decrease probably results from a general decline in volunteer
activity and the relatively strong cynicism felt toward politicians and
parties in the past decade. A sense that local campaign activity is not
particularly rewarding may be a third factor. When local associations
were asked following the 1993 campaign to list the most important
activities performed by their volunteers, more than nine in ten named
canvassing, six in ten election-day get-out-the-vote activity, four in ten

fundraising, and an equal number named the putting up of yard signs. Only one in fifty mentioned policy development as an important activity engaged in by local campaign activists. Interested citizens, particularly those without a strong personal tie to a nominee, may not be interested in knocking on doors or erecting yard signs, given that they are afforded virtually no opportunity to influence the party's policy platform.

RELATIONSHIP TO THE CENTRAL CAMPAIGN

In the run-up to an election campaign, the central parties offer training to their local activists in campaign techniques. Whether at "Liberal Universities" or "Reform Colleges," national and provincial party operatives train grassroots volunteers on essential campaign practices such as raising campaign funds, establishing a campaign office, organizing a canvassing campaign, and mobilizing voters on election day. Parties typically run these sessions in the months leading up to an expected election call in all parts of the country.

Once nominated, candidates are often invited to "candidate school." The central party trains candidates on things like dealing with the media, putting together a campaign operation, and answering policy questions. While substantial time is spent ensuring candidates understand the party's policy program, candidates have no real opportunity to influence policy. At one candidate training session, I witnessed a long conversation regarding a federal party's position on official bilingualism. Candidates took the opportunity to express their frustration with the party's position, claiming it was unpopular with many of their voters. While the exercise may have been cathartic for the candidates, the central party organizers only worried that it set them behind schedule. They had no apparent interest in their candidates' views on the issue. Rather, their concern was that candidates understood the party position and expressed it clearly to the local media or voters. Anyone who has ever attended an all-candidates debate during a federal or provincial election has witnessed candidates on the dais quickly poring through policy binders provided by their central party in order to answer a question on a particular topic. Candidates often recite the party's policy verbatim from the binder, occasionally with the appearance of reading it for the first time themselves.

However, there is some room for local exceptionalism in terms of policy. While candidates are not generally free to publicly distance themselves from the positions taken by their party and leader (in fact, they can face disciplinary action including dismissal as a candidate if they do), they are free to decide which issues to highlight in their campaigns, and occasionally local issues arise that are not on their national party's radar screen. Some local candidates create advertising and canvassing pieces in addition to those offered by the central party. While the national party seeks conformity and control over the activities of local candidates, central campaign officials acknowledge that occasions do arise where local candidates require some flexibility. For example, in the 1997 election supporters of the CBC attempted to make an issue out of government cuts to the public broadcaster. While this issue was not nationally important, it did gain some traction in a few urban centres. Some candidates endorsed by the Friends of the CBC highlighted this endorsement in their local campaign efforts.

The overriding concern for the central party in these instances is that the candidate not embarrass the party or the leader by emphasizing an issue the national party would rather not discuss during the campaign. The Reform Party often suggested to its candidates that they not emphasize the party's conservative social positions in their campaigns. While the central party was not running away from its positions, its strategists believed that highlighting these issues made electoral growth in targeted areas in Ontario more difficult by playing into its opponents' portrayal of the party as "too extreme."

Like a franchise operation, central parties not only create the substance of each candidate's campaign (the policy platform) but also control the outward appearance of the campaign (for more on the idea of parties as franchises, see Carty 2002). Materials such as yard signs, direct mail leaflets, brochures for door-to-door canvassing, and scripts for telephone canvassing are often centrally produced and sold to local campaigns. The purchase of these materials is often mandatory and costs local campaigns thousands of dollars. Included in these election services packages are computer software programs for organization of voter contact and get-out-the-vote efforts (discussed below).

POLLING

Most local campaigns do not engage in scientific public opinion polling. This is largely an issue of cost. A professional poll at the riding level with a sample size of a few hundred voters would normally cost over $10,000. This is simply out of reach for most candidates. Pollsters from all parties indicate that they discourage candidates from spending their scarce campaign resources on polls, primarily because of the costs and the fact that candidates have little scope to vary their campaigns on the basis of a poll's findings. Unlike the central party, the candidate cannot shape the policy platform or the message to be delivered in campaign advertisements.

In exceptional cases, local polling information can be helpful. For instance, in the Toronto riding of Broadview-Greenwood in 1988, the race was a contest between the New Democrat incumbent, Lynn McDonald, and the Liberal challenger. A poll conducted for the Liberal candidate, Dennis Mills, revealed that voters knew little about the New Democrat's opposition to Canada's continued participation in NATO. When voters were informed of this, however, a substantial number said it would make them less likely to support the incumbent. The issue, of little importance in the national campaign, had particular salience in this riding because of a large Greek community that supported NATO as a check on possible Turkish aggression. Mills used this polling data and highlighted the NDP position on NATO in his communication with ethnic voters in his successful campaign.

While professional polling is not a standard part of local campaigns, the central campaign conducts polls in ridings of particular importance to a party's overall strategy. For example, in recent elections the central NDP campaign has polled in the three to four dozen ridings where it thought the party was competitive. In effect these ridings constitute the universe of voters the national campaign is interested in communicating with, and accordingly it is essential to know what these voters are thinking and how they are reacting as the campaign unfolds. Similarly, the Liberals polled in all four Prince Edward Island ridings throughout the 1997 campaign. The ridings were tightly contested, and the central party believed victory in them was essential to putting together enough seats for majority status. Despite such extensive polling by the national parties, few local campaigns report that the national campaign shares any polling results with them. National campaign operatives suggest that their polling results are of little value to local campaigns, which are not normally expected to tailor the central campaign message in any event.

REACHING LOCAL VOTERS

Local campaigns regularly expend considerable energies on canvassing voters and erecting yard signs at the homes of identified supporters. For decades every campaign has included a "sign team." Volunteers deliver yard signs bearing the candidate's name along with the party's logo and official colours to the homes of supporters. Apartment dwellers place them in their windows and homeowners have them erected in their front lawns. One group of retirement-age volunteers spoke of picking up a list of supporters and dozens of signs at campaign headquarters every morning and spending a good portion of each campaign day delivering and erecting the signs. Many veteran local campaign volunteers claim the number of signs a candidate has up on private property is a good indication of her level of support and is important in creating a bandwagon effect. Undecided local voters, they claim, will be positively influenced by a predominance of signs for one candidate. There is, however, no scientific evidence that yard signs have any effect on the outcome of elections. One central campaign operative called these efforts "harmless," and justified them as providing a way for interested volunteers to get involved in the campaign. Similarly, an experienced local campaign operative suggested that erecting signs was a useful way of getting volunteers out of the office, where they can sometimes become a nuisance to those engaged in other campaign activities.

Canvassing is a more crucial part of local campaign efforts. Given its perceived importance in achieving electoral success (for which there is some compelling evidence; see Carty and Eagles forthcoming), the central parties have worked to develop more effective methods. Canvassing techniques and strategies are an integral part of the parties' campaign training schools. The central parties believe that, properly done, canvassing can persuade some undecided voters to vote for their candidate and is also an effective method of priming their own supporters to actually get to the polls and vote. As voter turnout continues to decline, these get-out-the-vote activities are increasingly important and can prove decisive. The key to success in canvassing is for local volunteers to deliver the right messages to the right voters.

Not many elections ago, the typical canvassing strategy consisted of trying to reach every voter with either a standard piece of campaign literature at their doorstep or a standard message over the telephone. Local volunteers would post street maps of the riding in the campaign office and colour in each neighbourhood as it was canvassed. The objective was to shade in the entire map before election day.

Today, parties focus their canvassing efforts on particular groups of voters and attempt to deliver a campaign message (or often a series of messages) of particular importance to those voters. Central party operatives instruct local volunteers on the importance of identifying swing areas of a riding (those with a large number of persuadable voters) and targeting them in their canvassing campaigns. Regional campaign operatives, hired by the central party, work closely with targeted riding campaigns to ensure the "right" voters are reached in the canvassing efforts. Their decisions are based on Statistics Canada data and polling data collected by the central party. Software programs are now used by all parties to facilitate delivery of targeted messages. (Of course, incumbents have more stable local campaign teams who are less in need of, and occasionally resent, instruction from the central campaign.)

The central parties' pollsters discern which groups of voters are of interest to the party. These are typically swing voters – undecided voters who are open to the possibility of supporting the party. Pollsters cannot identify individual swing voters, but they can identify sociodemographic groups with a heavy concentration of a party's swing voters. Sociodemographic profiles of Canadians by postal code, released by Statistics Canada, then allow a campaign to locate postal codes (representing discrete geographic areas) with a high concentration of these groups. For example, a pollster might determine that senior citizens should be the target of a party's communication strategy on the basis that they are interested in the party's prescription drug plan policy but are mostly not yet committed to any party. Statistics Canada data are then utilized to identufy neighbourhoods with a large concentration of elderly voters. The job for the local campaign then is to communicate with these senior citizens about prescription drug coverage. A well-run local campaign canvasses each group of targeted voters (there are normally several for each party) with the message that their party pollster determines to be particularly salient for each class of voters. This is one example of polling done at the national level that is of use to local campaigns. While all local campaigns will be trained in these techniques, regional and provincial party staff will work most closely with volunteers in a party's targeted ridings to implement the canvassing strategy.

Similarly, regional campaign staff work with ridings to develop effective plans for turning out their partisans on election day. These efforts are aimed at voters who are already committed supporters of the party. The logic is that if they turn out to vote they will vote for their party. They need not be persuaded, but rather mobilized. These contacts are made closer to voting day itself and usually consist of a reminder to vote and information as to where the voter's polling location is. Again polling data is useful. A pollster may determine that seniors are strong supporters of a party's leader. Local campaigns may be advised not to spend considerable time trying to persuade seniors (who in large numbers are already committed supporters) but rather to organize car pools and the like to make sure they vote. Again, local

campaigns that are winnable can expect significantly greater involvement from outside the riding than can those with little chance
for success.

The techniques described above group voters into sociodemographic clusters and thus have some limitations. Not all seniors, for
example, are primarily concerned with prescription drug costs. Some
are environmental activists while others' first concern may be issues
of law and order. By targeting any one sociodemographic group with a
single message there is sure to be some slippage – cases of the wrong
message being delivered to the wrong voters. Similarly, seniors do not
live only next-door to other seniors. Thus even if all seniors were interested in the same issue, a canvassing strategy that targets particular
neighbourhoods because of their high concentration of seniors is certain also to catch some young families and single people with very different political priorities. To deal with such slippage, parties are
developing new, more sophisticated methods that allow delivery of
personalized messages to individual voters.

New Campaign Technology

In recent campaigns the central parties have spent considerable time
developing, and teaching local campaigns how to implement, strategies for delivery of personalized messages to targeted voters. These
efforts revolve around sophisticated voter identification software
packages that allow local campaigns to build electronic files on potentially all voters. Beginning with the 1993 election, Elections Canada
has provided the parties with an electronic list of voters' names and
addresses in each riding. The parties have added information to this
computerized list in an attempt to ultimately create an individualized
profile of each voter. Some of the information is purchased, such as
electronic lists of phone numbers, and merged with the data provided
by Elections Canada. The parties already have other information on
voters: lists of those who took a yard sign or volunteered in the past
election, and of voters who have contacted the party with a concern
since the past campaign. This is particularly useful for incumbents,

who can track which voters have contacted them or their office with a policy question or to express their view on an issue. This information is then added to the voter's data file.

In practice this means that if a voter contacts her opposition member of Parliament to express her concerns with the government's support for the Kyoto environmental accord, the member can have this information recorded on the voter's electronic file. Then, come election time, the local campaign can call up all the files which note concern regarding the Kyoto Accord and send these voters a targeted mailing detailing the candidate's and party's environmental position. This voter's next-door neighbour, who called the same MP with concerns regarding gun control, can expect that issue to be the subject of the communication he receives during the campaign.

When party volunteers canvass voters during the course of a campaign and ask what issues they are interested in, voter responses are now routinely marked on bar code scan sheets and entered into the data files. The result is similar to that described above. A voter who in week two of the campaign tells the canvasser that she is particularly concerned with educational issues will have this noted on her electronic file and can expect to receive a mailing outlining the party's educational policy later in the campaign. This practice will become more and more sophisticated as local volunteers get used to its operation and continue to collect more data from election to election.

At the moment, these efforts are largely left to the local campaigns, with teaching and advice offered by the central campaign. However, it is easy to foresee, and indeed some campaign operatives suggest, that these canvassing efforts might be better run by experienced campaign professionals from a single central location – at least for those ridings the party believes to be most competitive. The central campaign might gather information on voters in key ridings in the months or even years leading up to an election campaign. The data might result from voter-initiated contact with the party, party surveying and canvassing of voters, and the increased amount of personal electronic data available for sale. The central campaign can then use these data to direct personalized messages to voters through direct mail and centralized phone banks.

Central control of the process also addresses one of the concerns expressed by party operatives regarding the potential of these techniques. They fear that the substantial turnover in local campaign personnel between elections means that data collected in one election may be lost by the time of the next election (or be in the attic of a volunteer from the last campaign who is no longer involved with the party). Similarly, party operatives worry that because many volunteers are working in their first campaign, they are unfamiliar with both the potential and the application of the software. Valuable campaign time is spent convincing local campaigns of the value of these techniques and then teaching them how to use the software. Some parties have already experimented with centralized projects aimed at delivering targeted messages into key ridings, and there is every reason to believe that this practice will continue and expand (see Lee 1989).

One campaign activity that has become increasingly regionalized and centralized in recent elections is the phone bank. Along with the door-to-door canvass, the phone bank has long been at the centre of local volunteer campaign efforts. For generations, local candidates' offices have included a handful of phone lines that are used by volunteers for canvassing voters. In the course of a couple of hours in the evening or on a Saturday afternoon, each volunteer might speak with as many as twenty-five voters. Volunteers read a phone script, often sent from party headquarters and adapted to include the name of the local candidate. While these local phone banks still exist, they have been replaced in importance and effectiveness by regional, automated calling centres.

In recent campaigns parties have established regional calling centres with dozens of phone lines, automated calling machines, and operators. Central party officials identify key ridings in their area and call into these constituencies. Using automated dialling systems, like those used by telemarketing firms, that immediately patch calls through to an operator when a live person answers, each operator can speak to more than 100 voters in the course of an evening. Even more voters can be reached using pre-recorded messages, often from the party's leader. Local ridings regularly lobby regional and central campaign staff to have calls made into their ridings. Consistent with the general interest of the central campaign in local efforts, priority is always given to those constituencies targeted by the central campaign as winnable.

The National Campaign

Occurring at the same time as the 301 local campaigns is a national campaign centred on the parties' leaders. Central parties typically spend limited time and resources on local efforts as their focus is overwhelmingly on the national campaign. This campaign involves public opinion polling, the leader's tour, debate preparation, mass media advertising, and media management. Central campaigns concentrate their energies and resources on these activities, believing that campaigns are won and lost on their successful execution.

CAMPAIGN PERSONNEL

The central campaigns are not participatory exercises; rather, they are dominated by a small group of seasoned campaigners and close associates of the party leaders. In most parties, the central operatives who run the party's extraparliamentary affairs between elections are pushed aside come election time. Two groups tend to take over the parties' central operations during election campaigns: individuals with long-standing connections to the party leader, and experienced professionals with particular campaign-related skills. More than one senior party official talks about the parties' having peacetime and wartime generals. The peacetime generals are the loyal party apparatchiks who organize party conventions, oversee non-campaign-year fundraising, service the party membership and riding associations, and generally keep the party headquarters functioning between election campaigns. The wartime generals take over to run the campaigns.

Many of the wartime generals will have worked with the party leader during the leadership campaign. These organizers and strategists will have earned the leader's trust during these very personal campaigns. In a sense these individuals form a personal entourage of experienced campaigners whose first loyalty is to the leader. They are often joined during the election by other seasoned party campaigners who may not have close ties to the leader but tend to have necessary expertise (for example, a pollster, an advertising executive, a media-time buyer). Normally, those who have been with the leader for a long period of time will form the campaign's inner circle, with other party campaign professionals filling the second tier and the party's inter-election staff often relegated to the outer circle.

The wartime generals are almost never employed by the party during nonelection periods. In the case of the governing party, they may be in the prime minister's office or other senior political positions. In the Liberal and Conservative parties many of these loyalists have been rewarded with Senate seats when their party was in power. Long-time Liberal campaign strategists Keith Davey, Jerry Grafstein, and more recently Chrétien operative David Smith, and Conservatives Marjory LeBreton and Lowell Murray are examples. Other wartime generals work for public affairs and consulting firms in Ottawa. Firms such as Hill and Knowlton or Ottawa's Earnscliffe Group are typical homes for party strategists between election periods. Many of these firms are bipartisan in that they house key campaign strategists for more than one party. For example, in the course of researching this book I interviewed senior advisors to both the Liberal and Conservative campaigns who were employed with the Earnscliffe Group. Obviously, this is an advantage to the firms as they can advertise to clients that they have connections with various political parties and essentially cover their bases no matter who wins a particular election.

Other senior strategists are drawn from the business and legal worlds. Examples of this are long-time Chrétien advisors (and senior

Liberal campaign strategists) John Rae and David Smith. Rae is a senior executive with the Power Corporation who regularly found time to help Chrétien during election campaigns. Similarly, before his appointment to the Senate, Smith was managing partner with a large Toronto-based law firm who took substantial time away from his legal practice during election campaigns.

These folks are not in politics for financial gain. In fact, they lose substantial amounts of money from their private enterprises when they engage in political campaign activity. They participate for a number of reasons. Most have close personal ties to the leader they serve. Many simply enjoy politics and, as more than one mentioned, "the adrenaline rush of competition" it brings is unlike anything in the private sector. All of these men and women (though most are men) talk about their political activity as a form of public service. In listening to these individuals it is clear that they believe deeply in government (many are former political aides and public servants) and believe their largely volunteer campaign activity contributes to Canadian society. Of course, those employed in consulting and public affairs firms have some pecuniary interest; they can trade on their political connections in seeking private-sector clients and in competing for government contracts should their side win.

Those providing professional skills to the campaign, such as the pollsters and the creative advertising team, essentially move to the campaign from their private-sector businesses. They are not employees of the party but hired guns for the duration of the campaign. There are not enough elections in Canada to allow these professionals to work exclusively, or even primarily, on election campaigns. (This is unlike the situation in the United States, where a plethora of state and federal elections supports a permanent campaign industry.) The pollsters and creative teams typically have their own private practices, and the vast majority of their work (and income) comes from the private sector. Pollsters often engage in interelection polling for the parties or even for the government, but this represents a tiny portion of their overall business. For advertisers, the possibility of winning government contracts is a more significant enticement, as the federal and provincial governments are among the country's largest advertisers. Of course, in recent federal campaigns this incentive would exist only for Liberal Party supporters.

Like those working in consulting and public affairs firms, pollsters do benefit professionally from association with a political party. For example, several talked about the prestige of being the pollster for a major political party. They believe they are looked up to by their professional peers and that the public recognition of being a party pollster assists them in attracting private sector clients. All in all, however, it appears that their desire to be involved in public affairs, their commitment to a particular party or leader, and their love of politics are the key factors motivating their political activity. Several of these political professionals speak about politics using war metaphors, and the campaign's nerve centre is often called the "war room." (Several senior operatives are amateur war historians, and at least one has an expensive-looking mock battlefield in his office.) Participation in the inner circle of political campaigns provides these men with an excitement not found in their routine business lives. The old saying that "politics is the only sport for adults" resonates with these folks, who seem to enjoy the sport of politics as much as its public policy outcomes.

CAMPAIGN STRATEGIES

Canada's first-past-the-post, single-member constituency electoral system dictates the parties' campaign strategies. Electoral competition is shaped by the reality that winners are declared in each of 301 separate contests, and that the victorious party is the one that wins a plurality of the vote in a plurality of these contests. Elections are not necessarily won by the party winning the most votes. As recently as 1979, the federal Liberals' share of the popular vote exceeded the Conservatives' by almost five percentage points, yet the Conservatives won the election (provincial governments in the 1990s in British Columbia, Saskatchewan, and Quebec were all elected with fewer votes than the party finishing second). Similarly, in both 1993 and 1997 the Conservatives won a similar proportion of the vote to the Reform

Party, yet Reform won many more seats. The reason for these apparent discrepancies is that some votes are "worth" more than others. The Canadian electoral system favours voters who share a political interest with others who live close by. Concentrated in a single city, 30,000 Reformers can elect an MP, while 30,000 Conservatives spread throughout a province cannot (see Courtney 2004).

Accordingly, the first strategic imperative for a party is to identify the ridings where it has a chance to win a plurality of the vote. No benefit is accorded a campaign that finishes a strong second in a riding; the result is the same as finishing a distant fifth. An efficient campaign therefore concentrates on the ridings where the party has a realistic chance to finish first, and is not concerned with the others. These strategies are not unique to Canada. Many of the techniques used by the parties to identify their targeted ridings and voters were developed in the United States (Sabato 1981) and are now widely used in Western democracies with first-past-the post electoral systems. For example, in recent British elections, Whiteley and Seyd (2003) have identified an increase in parties' targeting their electoral efforts to marginal ridings while minimizing their efforts elsewhere.

In the current Canadian party system this means dramatically different things to different parties. For more than a hundred years from Confederation to 1993, each election began with two parties competing for majority status. Each concentrated on some parts of the country more than others, but neither could ignore large sections, because they regularly sought to win a majority of the country's ridings. This is no longer the case. In recent elections, only the Liberal Party has begun the campaign with the realistic objective of winning a majority of the ridings. The other four principal parties set significantly lower goals. Using the example of the 2000 election (though 1997 was similar), the Canadian Alliance was focused on holding onto its base in western Canada and trying to make a significant breakthrough in Ontario. The Conservatives and New Democrats were both trying to elect their leaders and at least eleven other candidates, to guarantee them official party status in the House of Commons. The Bloc

Québécois, of course, contested elections only in Quebec and spent no resources outside the province.

The Canadian parties rely on their pollsters to identify the ridings and regions of the country where they have sufficient voter support to stand a chance of finishing first in individual ridings. The parties regularly conduct large baseline polls in the weeks and months leading up to an election campaign in order to identify these regions. Many ridings are then dismissed from the central party's campaign efforts. Again using the 2000 campaign for illustrative purposes, the Conservatives discovered that they were competitive in much of Atlantic Canada, isolated pockets in Quebec and rural southwestern Ontario, and in one riding in each of Manitoba (Brandon-Souris) and Alberta (Calgary Centre). As Peter Woolstencroft (2001, 99) points out, "Although the rhetoric of the party's leaders routinely referred to it as a national, political entity, the territorial focus at the outset of its campaign belied these pretensions." Similarly the New Democrats identified about three dozen ridings scattered across the country (concentrated in Atlantic Canada and the Prairies, with none in Quebec or Alberta; see Whitehorn 2001). Only the Liberals had aspirations of winning seats in most parts of the country, though even they held little hope of success in much of British Columbia and Alberta.

Beyond eliminating parts of the country where party strategists believe they have little chance of finishing first, the parties also identify areas of strong support where they stand little chance of *not* finishing first. The objective here is to ensure that scarce campaign resources are not wasted on running up large majorities in ridings that are safely in a party's column. Again, this strategy results from the workings of the electoral system, which awards the maximum benefit when a party receives one vote more than any of its opponents in a riding and offers no additional benefit for larger margins of victory. This fact is obviously of greater concern to parties such as the Liberals and Alliance in 2000, who were attempting to expand their bases and wished to focus their efforts on those marginal ridings where extra effort might result in victory. For example, the Alliance had many safe seats in Alberta and British Columbia in which it faced no real opposition. This allowed the party to expend few national campaign resources in these provinces and to direct them instead to potential growth areas, particularly in Ontario (Ellis 2001).

The net result of this regional targeting (which stems from the increase in the number of competitive parties and the resulting lowered electoral expectations for most of them) is that parties focus their campaign efforts on an ever declining number of ridings. The Conservatives and New Democrats have been competitive in so few ridings in recent elections that they have essentially run a series of concurrent by-election campaigns.

What is important from a democratic audit perspective is that this effect of the electoral system has dramatically regionalized electoral competition. When the Conservatives and Liberals dominated, they both campaigned across most parts of the country. Voters on the west coast, in the prairies, in the industrial heartland, in francophone Quebec, and in Atlantic Canada were all choosing between these two parties. From the 1960s onward this changed somewhat as the New Democrats built some areas of regional strength (primarily west of the Ottawa River). In the post-1993 party system, however, with five competitive parties, four of which have limited electoral appeal, and three of which are closely identified with particular regions (the Bloc with Quebec, the Alliance with the West, and the Conservatives with Atlantic Canada), Canadian politics have become extremely balkanized.

In both the 1997 and 2000 federal elections, voters experienced very different campaigns depending on where they lived in the country. As illustrated in Table 6.1, voters in Atlantic Canada were choosing between the Conservatives and Liberals, with the NDP competitive in Nova Scotia. Voters in Quebec witnessed a campaign between the Liberals and the Bloc, and Ontario was dominated by the Liberals, who faced a divided and thus electorally inefficient opposition. Manitoba voters came the closest of Canadians anywhere to having a competitive race between all of the major parties, as all except the Bloc had some degree of strength in the province. Voters in Saskatchewan were

Table 6.1

Party winning most votes in every province and any parties winning half as many votes as the first-place party, 1997 and 2000

	1997		2000	
	First place	Half as many votes	First place	Half as many votes
Newfoundland	Liberal	Conservative, New Democratic	Liberal	Conservative
Nova Scotia	Conservative	New Democratic, Liberal	Liberal	Conservative, New Democratic
Prince Edward Island	Liberal	Conservative	Liberal	Conservative
New Brunswick	Conservative	Liberal, New Democratic	Liberal	Conservative
Quebec	Bloc	Liberal, Conservative	Liberal	Bloc
Ontario	Liberal	—	Liberal	—
Manitoba	Liberal	Reform, New Democratic, Conservative	Liberal	Alliance, New Democratic
Saskatchewan	Reform	New Democratic, Liberal	Alliance	New Democratic
Alberta	Reform	—	Alliance	—
British Columbia	Reform	Liberal	Alliance	Liberal

choosing between the Alliance and the NDP. And the Alliance domi-nated Alberta and primarily faced the Liberals in British Columbia. Outside of Atlantic Canada, no two provinces in the 2000 campaign had the same set of competitive parties.

The regionalization of the campaign is reflected not only in the cast of parties competitive in each province but also in the campaign discourse. A campaign waged between the Conservatives and Liberals in Atlantic Canada will focus on different issues than one between the Alliance and Liberals in British Columbia. In recent campaigns, the parties have prepared different strategies and messages for different regions of the country. While, to a certain extent, the parties have always prepared different campaign strategies for English and French Canada, the degree of balkanization has increased dramatically in the last decade. This practice was most evident in the 1997 campaign. Shocked by the regional tenor of the 1993 campaign, the governing Lib-erals prepared very differently for the next election. Senior campaign officials with experience covering decades of federal elections claim that the party's regional approach to the election was unprecedented.

Knowing it would face different opponents from different sides of the political spectrum in different regions, the party essentially developed four or five distinct regional campaign plans. Different advertising was created and aired, different messages were developed, and essentially different campaigns waged in each region. Other parties took a similar approach. For example, the Conservatives attacked the Liberals from the left in Atlantic Canada and from the right in Ontario.

This fragmentation abated somewhat in the 2000 campaign. While the opposition parties still created regional plans, the electoral landscape allowed the Liberals to run a less regionally focused campaign than they had in 1997. Because the New Democrats and Conservatives were very weak entering the 2000 campaign and the Alliance was on an upswing in the immediate aftermath of the selection of a new leader, the Liberals were able to cast the campaign as a contest between themselves and the Alliance (Marzolini 2001). Essentially, they ignored the New Democrats and Conservatives by arguing that voters supporting either of these parties were increasing the likelihood of the Alliance winning. This strategy was wholly dependent on the weak electoral position of these two parties, the apparent surge in Alliance support, and the fact that NDP and Conservative voters preferred the Liberals to the Alliance. Should any of these factors change in future elections (which they almost surely will), we can expect the Liberals to revert to their 1997 approach of preparing different strategies for what is now essentially a multifront campaign. (For an opposing view on this subject, see Clarkson 2001.)

The parties' advertising reflects the increased importance of region to their electoral strategies. From the early 1950s to 1993, the parties used television primarily to deliver national advertising messages. Of course, French advertisements were created for francophone Quebec, but most of the advertising dollars were spent on nationwide advertising. This has changed dramatically. In the 2000 campaign the parties spent a majority of their advertising budgets on regionally targeted buys. For example, the Conservatives concentrated their television advertising in Ontario and Atlantic Canada. The New Democrats focused all of their advertising on the few dozen ridings they had hopes of winning. This meant they purchased no advertising on the national networks but used local television and relied heavily on local radio (Whitehorn 2001). The Alliance spent one-quarter of its advertising dollars on national advertisements and the remainder regionally. Even the Liberals, who claim to have run a national campaign, prepared some television advertisements for specific regional audiences and directed their advertising dollars to areas of the country where they thought they could make electoral gains.

While federal campaigns have taken on a regional hue, this has not shifted decision-making power away from the parties' central operatives to regional and local party officials. While parties are increasingly aiming their advertising at discrete regional groups, local campaign officials play no organized role in setting the advertising agenda. Central party operatives are hard-pressed when asked to identify the role local campaign officials play in setting and executing the national campaign strategy.

Once the parties have settled on the particular messages for each targeted group, their attention turns to methods of delivering the message. The proliferation of television channels over the past decade allows the parties to use this broadcast medium for "narrowcasting." Narrowcasting is the sending of tailored messages to specific groups of voters. The parties employ time buyers to identify which programs have high proportions of viewers from among their target groups. In a television universe with a multitude of channels, many of them specialized to appeal to specific demographic groups (such as sports channels, the Women's Television Network, religious channels, etc.), different programs have dramatically different audiences. This is a significant change from just a couple of decades ago when most Canadians had access to only three or four networks and most shows had a more diverse audience.

Today a party whose pollster suggests they target young men can air an advertisement with a message aimed at this group on an all-sports network and know with certainty that the audience will be dominated by young men. The same party may produce a separate spot aimed at stay-at-home moms and air it on a program such as *Martha*

Stewart Living with a large number of such women among its viewers. Radio is also widely used for targeted messages. Campaign advertisements in different languages are prepared for airing on radio stations whose audience is dominated by a particular minority group.

LEADERS' TOURS

As long as there have been federal election campaigns, the parties' leaders have toured the country seeking electoral support. In the very first campaigns after Confederation, voting was staggered, with the prime minister deciding when ridings held their elections. John A. Macdonald began his campaigns with voting in his home riding of Kingston, then moved his base to Toronto to campaign for the next round of votes. By the end of the nineteenth century, when voting dates were standardized, Prime Minister Laurier was touring the country by train, attending scores of events during each campaign. Since the advent of the airplane in the twentieth century, leaders have criss-crossed the country for the duration of election campaigns.

The leaders' tours are key parts of the parties' strategies because of the media they generate. The national press, feeling compelled to report on the election during each day of the campaign, relies on the leaders' tours for their stories. So the pictures voters see on the evening news and the stories they read in their morning newspapers often result from the tours. The campaigns devote enormous energy to scripting the leaders' events in an attempt to control the message the media delivers to voters.

Though the tour gives the appearance of bringing together the national and local campaigns, this is more mirage than reality. While the tour brings the party leaders to cities and towns across the country and presents the image of the leader meeting with local folks, listening to their concerns, and learning about local issues, in reality today's tours are highly scripted affairs with very little opportunity for accidental encounters between voters and party leaders.

The central parties see the leaders' tours as the centrepiece of their campaign efforts and the tours are orchestrated by experienced "wartime generals," such as the New Democrat Richard McLellan and the Liberal David Miller, for example. These men have deep roots in their respective parties. After decades of service to the party in different capacities, Miller has served as tour director for Jean Chrétien's campaigns. McLellan has been involved in NDP politics for an equally long period, and his experience with campaign tours dates back to the leadership of Tommy Douglas. Like most wartime generals they have other jobs between campaigns. Miller has served as a vice-president with the public relations firm Hill and Knowlton, and McLellan in the legislative office of the Ontario New Democrats.

The parties identify three objectives for the tours: to present a favourable image of their leader to voters; to deliver the party's message; and to reinforce its paid advertising. As with campaign advertising, region is important in tour planning. The leaders spend most of their time in their party's targeted regions, which are the same areas where it is advertising most heavily. For example, as noted above the Alliance was focusing on Ontario in the 2000 campaign, and leader Stockwell Day spent all or part of twenty-three days in Ontario out of the total thirty-one days that he spent campaigning. Similarly Alexa McDonough, whose New Democratic Party was focusing on Manitoba, Saskatchewan, and Nova Scotia, spent all or part of seven days in Manitoba and eight in each of the other two provinces. By comparison, Chrétien spent only three days each in Manitoba and Nova Scotia and four in Saskatchewan.

A party uses polling and focus group findings to determine the image of its leader that it wishes to present to voters, and then structures the tour to accomplish this objective. For example, in the lead-up to Chrétien's first campaign in 1993, senior Liberals were concerned that voters might perceive him as being too old and as "yesterday's man," given that he had been a highly visible figure in national politics for almost three decades. To dispel this perception they arranged for Chrétien to engage in vigorous activities during his tour. Party strategists were delighted when the national television networks' nightly campaign coverage included pictures of a fit-looking Chrétien helping Atlantic Canadian workers unload cases of beer from a delivery truck. The party also planned a full schedule of events for Chrétien most days, to help present the image of a vital leader.

The tour provides parties with an opportunity to get their policy messages out to voters. The hundreds of voters who may physically be in attendance at an event are less important than a party's targeted voters, at whom the message is aimed. They are reached by news coverage of the tour, which communicates a leader's words to Canadians across the country. The messages on the tour will often be chosen to complement a campaign's paid advertising. For example, if a party is running television advertisements claiming that its opponents have a weak record on the environment, its leader may highlight this subject when touring the parts of the country where these advertisements are running. The advertising message is thus reinforced on the evening news.

Once the central campaign determines the regions of the country to be visited and the subject matter to be highlighted, the exact location of a speech is often chosen for its connection to the message the leader is delivering. For example, an opposition leader's speech on health care reform may be given at a regional hospital with an overflowing outpatients ward or a long waiting list for elective surgery. The physical locale provides images that complement the party's message and makes it easy for television journalists accompanying the leader both to interview locals and to generally tell the story of a health care system in crisis.

Teams of advance persons, trained by the central party, arrive at the chosen sites days (and sometimes weeks) in advance of the leader. These central party operatives generally have absolute control over the leaders' events. The parties have detailed manuals and checklists that their advance teams use in preparing for the leader's arrival. They ensure that crowds are arranged for, that all of the logistics of the event are tended to, and if the event is indoors that the room is an appropriate size. They drive the route the leader is to take when in town and check with local highway officials to ensure no construction work is planned. No detail is overlooked. Many of these concerns are the results of prior disasters. Party folklore is full of tales of microphones that didn't work, rooms far too large for the crowd attracted, buses too tall to fit under highway overpasses, and events beginning hours late.

One of the parties' greatest fears is that these types of mishap will be reported by the press as evidence of a party in disarray. They fear voters will conclude that a party that cannot organize a successful tour is incapable of organizing a government. There are recent examples of parties falling victim to these perceptions. In the 2000 campaign Alliance leader Stockwell Day used the backdrop of the Niagara River to criticize the governing Liberals for the alleged "brain drain" to the United States. Day argued that like the river, Canadian talent was flowing into the United States. The problem, quickly picked up on (and widely reported) by the media, was that the river flows over Niagara Falls (not up it) and thus into and not out of Canada. This may seem like a minor faux pas, but it dogged the campaign for several days and was used as evidence of an inept party organization and leader. Similarly, media reports of Bloc leader Gilles Duceppe's campaign bus being lost in rural Quebec were turned into a metaphor for a directionless campaign.

Party strategists increasingly try to script every movement of the tour to eliminate spontaneity. This is an attempt to control the message the media reports from the tour. If the planners succeed at presenting the leader only in the manner they desire, giving the scripted message and surrounded by cheering supporters, they can be confident that the pictures and sound bite on that evening's newscast will be what they are hoping for. On the other hand, if the leader is surrounded by hecklers and is thrown off-message by media questions or a hostile crowd, these events are likely to be the focus of the media coverage, with little attention paid to the planned issue of the day. The result is what is referred to as the "bubble strategy." Party leaders arrive at staged events in carefully selected locations filled with local supporters, give their prepared remarks, then quickly exit to the cheers of the supportive crowd. Increasingly, party operatives work to avoid opportunities for unscripted chance encounters between the leader and voters. The fear is that real voters are unpredictable and that the press will report on these spontaneous encounters rather than the carefully planned and scripted official events.

LEADERS' DEBATES

The one hiatus in the tour occurs in the days leading up to the leaders' debates. In the words of one seasoned campaign veteran, these debates have taken on "mythical proportions." Debates between party leaders have been an integral part of Canadian election campaigns for more than twenty years. While there is no provision in law requiring participation, all of the major parties believe there would be serious voter backlash should they choose not to participate. The parties treat these events as crucial to their chances of electoral success. Data from various Canadian election studies suggest that while debates sometimes do have a significant impact on voting behaviour, the campaign operative quoted above is probably correct in suggesting that their importance is often overestimated (Johnston et al. 1992; Blais et al. 2002).

Nonetheless, debates do provide most voters with their only extended, unmediated exposure to the party leaders. Lasting an average of 90 to 120 minutes, debates provide the leaders with an unparalleled opportunity to communicate their policy views to voters and, equally important, to present themselves in a favourable way to the electorate. Party strategists focus on both substance and style in debate preparations.

The parties expend considerable time and resources negotiating every last detail of the debates' organization and preparing their leaders for the event. The subjects to be covered in the debate are normally determined through negotiations between party strategists and the television networks. Therefore the parties can generally anticipate what issues will be covered. The key for the party leader, according to several senior strategists, is to smoothly bridge from the question asked in a particular subject area to the message on the subject that the party wishes to communicate to voters. Extensive effort goes into preparing the exact wording of a party's message on each of the agreed-upon themes. These phrases and paragraphs are often subject to extensive testing including evaluation by focus groups of voters prior to the debate. Pollsters also weigh in with advice on what messages should be highlighted in order for the leader to appeal to the party's targeted voters.

Party strategists attempt to take the risk out of these debates by scripting their leader as much as possible. This is not to suggest that the leaders simply repeat the words put into their mouths by the strategists. In fact, leaders often play a key role in composing the message. The point is that many of the sentences and paragraphs that come out of the leaders' mouths during a debate (often with the appearance of spontaneity) have been carefully prepared and tested with voters beforehand. Strategists for a party with a lead in the polls will want to minimize opportunities for unscripted and thus unpredictable moments in the debate. In negotiations over the format they will argue for set pieces, such as longer opening and closing remarks that are prepared in advance, questions and answers with journalists with no opportunity for follow-up questions, and limited opportunity for free-for-all debate among the candidates. Parties are never able to completely eliminate unscripted segments, however, and these often constitute the most memorable moments of a debate.

Significant attention is also paid to the leaders' debating style. The parties believe that voters use debates to judge the leaders' personalities and character as much as their policy positions. Therefore leaders routinely engage in mock debates against stand-ins acting as leaders of the opposing parties. Tapes of these encounters are shown to focus groups who are asked their view on things such as how likeable, trustworthy, and honest the leader appears. Media experts are employed to work with the leaders to ensure that their mannerisms and style result in the desired image. Female leaders face unique obstacles in this regard. They often believe they need to be assertive in style to show that they are "tough enough" for the job, yet they risk being perceived as shrill and overly aggressive by the media. Research findings show that the media often exaggerate the assertiveness of female candidates in leaders' debates (Gidengil and Everitt 2002). The right balance can prove an elusive goal.

While millions of Canadians watch the nationally televised debates live (in recent campaigns there has been one debate in each official language), many others form their opinion based on media reports. The result is that party strategists work hard in the lead-up to the debates lowering expectations for their leader and arguing afterward that he performed better than expected. While stopping short of calling their leader a dullard, they often exaggerate the cleverness and debating experience of his opponents while referring to their leader as a folksy, regular fellow without a silver tongue.

Auditing Election Campaigning

In terms of the Audit benchmarks of participation, inclusiveness, and responsiveness, voters have different experiences of election campaigns depending on the competitiveness of the riding they live in. Supporters of the New Democrats and Conservatives were able to participate at the highest levels and have considerable discretion in the type of campaign waged in most constituencies in recent elections. This was because these parties had no hope of winning in most ridings and were happy simply to locate a candidate and enough local volunteers to mount a campaign. The situation is similar for Liberal, Alliance, and Bloc supporters in ridings where their party is not competitive. The central party offices expend few resources and pay little attention to what the locals do in these ridings. However, in those ridings where a party is competitive, central party operatives follow the local campaign closely and work to ensure that their campaign strategy and plans are implemented in the constituency. Local party members have no similar opportunity to influence the national campaign strategy.

In addition to concentrating their efforts on particular ridings, parties are increasingly targeting particular groups of voters within these ridings. Sophisticated uses of public opinion polling and new communications technology allow the parties to deliver tailored messages to discrete groups of voters. Parties are now trying to take this to the next level by creating individualized voter files that allow the delivery of personalized messages to all targeted voters. Both of these phenomena, the increased targeting of particular ridings and targeting of subgroups of voters within these ridings, are encouraged by the highly fragmented Canadian party system. With five major parties competing for votes in contemporary federal elections, the percentage of votes needed for success is substantially less than half. Parties need not speak to, and attempt to persuade, a majority of voters, but can concentrate on the small block of swing voters crucial to their efforts. In doing so, the parties are becoming increasingly dependent on campaign professionals such as pollsters and media-time buyers at the expense of more traditional, volunteer-intensive techniques such as door-to-door canvassing. Given the decline in person-to-person communication, one must wonder whether there is a connection between the changing nature of election campaigning and declining voter turnout.

The lasting result of these changes is the decline of pan-Canadian election campaigning. If election campaigns once offered opportunity for national debate on the pressing issues of the day, this is no longer the case. Today voters in different regions of the country hear from different parties during election campaigns. The result is that some issues dominate political discourse in one region while being barely mentioned in another. And the workings of the first-past-the-post electoral system lead the central parties to essentially write off all those ridings where they have no chance of winning a plurality of the vote. Rather than one national campaign, today's federal elections have become little more than a series of regional by-elections. This minimizes the emergence of national debate and consensus. Therefore elections do not provide an opportunity for Canadians to send a clear message to their political parties, and parties have little opportunity to receive strong mandates from voters. On the positive side, this lack of central party interest gives substantial authority to the parties' local activists. On the negative side, volunteers in these ridings are engaged in activity that has no influence whatsoever on the election's overall result. Like so much of party decision making, the more consequential the activity, the less room there is for meaningful grassroots involvement.

All of this election activity, at both the local and national levels, is increasingly expensive. The next chapter examines the financing of the parties' campaign activities.

Chapter 6

Election Campaigning

Strengths

- Canadian federal elections comprise 301 local campaigns, providing significant opportunity for grassroots participation in election activity.

- Parties are the key players in election campaigns, structuring electoral competition and organizing voter participation and choice.

Weaknesses

- Central parties are increasingly dependent on political professionals, such as pollsters and advertising specialists, and are relying less on person-to-person techniques such as door-to-door canvassing.

- Canadian campaigns are becoming increasingly regionalized and fragmented, diminishing opportunity for national consensus building and mandates.

- The first-past-the-post electoral system means that party volunteers in many ridings are engaged in "no-hope" campaigns that have no impact on election results.

7   MONEY AND POLITICS

That money is a necessary part of political campaigns in Canada is undeniable. Election campaigns are fundamentally about communication among parties, candidates, and voters. In a country as large and diverse as Canada this is necessarily an expensive endeavour. Accordingly, money has been called both the mother's milk of politics and the fuel that nourishes politics. However, the relationship between money and politics is in fact more complex than providing energy or sustenance. A less benign analogy is that the attraction between money and politics is an addiction, as politicians appear to need continuously more funds for their ever more expensive campaigns, and regulatory efforts to control money in politics are routinely subverted by ever more creative methods on the part of those dependent on it.

Left unchecked, money can distort electoral democracy by favouring the candidates and parties with access to substantial resources. The influence of campaign financing outlasts the election cycle, as successful candidates are often later accused of being overly responsive to those who provided their campaign funds. While money is certainly a catalyst for the growth and development of the political system, campaign finance abuses are a poisonous drug eating away at the fundamental assumptions that justify citizens' faith in politics.

Recognizing the importance of regulating money in the electoral process, Canadian governments have enacted a series of regulatory measures from shortly after Confederation to the present day. The most comprehensive effort to regulate political financing took place in 1974 with the adoption of the Canada Elections Act. This legislation remained the basic framework for the regulation of campaign financing until the Liberal government adopted significant reforms in 2003. The new legislation has yet to be tested in an election cycle, and thus its impact is still largely hypothetical. This makes an examination of Canadian party and election financing more difficult. Nonetheless, this chapter includes an examination of the state of campaign financing in recent election cycles, highlights the impetuses for reform, identifies the changes in the new legislation, and suggests what some of their important implications may be.

The distinguished student of Canadian politics Khayyam Paltiel (1987, 228) identified three objectives underlying campaign finance regulation: probity and transparency in order to preserve voter confidence that the system is free of corruption and quid pro quo arrangements; equity to ensure a balanced playing field among parties and candidates with none vastly outspending the others; and accessibility to electoral competition for all citizens regardless of their financial status. These criteria are consistent with the Audit's benchmarks of responsiveness, inclusiveness, and participation. A participatory and inclusive political system must offer citizens of different political persuasions the opportunity to successfully compete for political office without undue regard to their access to material wealth. Similarly, a participatory and responsive politics can only flourish if office holders are not beholden to corporations, labour unions, or other special interests for the funds necessary to be elected. Probity and transparency are required so voters know who is funding the parties' campaigns and so that violations of any regulations are brought to light.

There is an alternative view of campaign finance regulation (see, for example, Palda 1991). This view rejects regulatory efforts to create a level playing field and to limit the amounts candidates raise and spend. Its proponents advocate a free-market approach checked only by full disclosure. Supporters of this view argue that candidates and parties should be able to raise unlimited funds from any source and to spend as much as they wish on their campaign efforts. Full disclosure of the parties' and candidates' finances, they argue, allows voters to act as a check on these activities at the ballot box, making other regulation unnecessary. This approach has traditionally been rejected in Canada primarily because it does nothing to increase accessibility and competitiveness in political competition; those with access to great wealth could drown out the voices of those with limited means. Such a system also provides no incentives for candidates and parties to raise funds from ordinary voters and provides no check on their reliance on special interests for campaign funds. Concerns for participatory, inclusive, and responsive politics argue against such a system.

Probity and Transparency

The Canadian regulatory scheme attempts to achieve transparency and probity through comprehensive disclosure requirements and limitations on who can contribute to campaigns. According to the disclosure provisions,

* Candidates and parties must report the amount and source of all contributions, and the names and addresses of those whose contributions exceed $200.
* Parties and candidates must disclose how their campaign funds are spent.
* Disclosure reports from candidates must be submitted within four months of a general election and from parties within six months.

The limitations on contribution sources provide that

* Individuals who are not citizens or permanent residents of Canada are not permitted to make any contributions to parties or candidates.

- Corporations and trade unions are prohibited from making any contributions to parties, and contributions to candidates are limited to $1,000 per calendar year.
- Contributions from individuals to parties and candidates are limited to $5,000 per calendar year.

Requiring disclosure of all contributions in excess of $200 means that any interested Canadian can easily discover the source of parties' and candidates' funding. Elections Canada now posts all of the relevant information on the Internet. Although the information is not posted in an easily accessible format, with a little perseverance interested voters can find a complete list of contribution sources. While no system can prevent all deliberate acts of subversion, the Canada Elections Act includes enforcement provisions that provide reasonable assurance that parties and candidates are complying with the disclosure requirements.

The disclosure requirements are effective in providing information to the public on who funded the campaigns and allowing the media and opposition to serve as watchdogs checking whether large contributors are later favoured by the government. However, the disclosure requirements fall short in one significant respect: all of the reporting is done postelection. This means that none of this information is available to voters while considering which candidate and party to vote for. One purpose of disclosure requirements is that they provide voters with additional information about a party or candidate's allies, that is, from whom they raise their campaign funds. Knowing that a party raises a significant portion of its funds from the oil industry, pro-life organizations, the tobacco industry, the trial lawyers association, or environmentalists might form an important part of voters' calculus in deciding whom to vote for. This information is not available to Canadian voters until months after the election, too late to influence the campaign for which the funds were solicited and years before the next election.

Pre-election disclosure is possible, and is a key part of the campaign finance system in the United States. Pre-election disclosure routinely allows US candidates to take issue with the source of an opponent's campaign funding and enables the media to keep a critical eye on candidates' fundraising activities during the course of a campaign. The 2000 presidential campaign provided an example of this. Republican John McCain focused much of his primary campaign on the need for campaign finance reform. He charged that the system, in which candidates were heavily reliant on corporate and trade union contributions, encouraged successful candidates to be overly responsive to these special interests once in office. McCain's campaign suffered when it was revealed that he was raising substantial funds from companies regulated by the Senate commerce committee that he chaired.

Some party officials argue that pre-election disclosure is administratively burdensome. It is difficult to see the merit in this argument. If a party can solicit a contribution, process the cheque, take the cheque to the bank and cash it, and spend the money before the election, surely it can find the time to post the contribution on its website or in some other generally accessible form.

Prior to the 2003 legislation, the federal limitations on who could contribute to parties and candidates essentially prohibited contributions from foreign interests while allowing virtually all else. The result, as illustrated in Tables 7.1 and 7.2, was that parties and candidates received a significant portion of their funding from corporations and trade unions. The governing Liberals received approximately six of every ten dollars raised in the 2000 election cycle from corporations. The Conservatives raised half their funds and the Alliance one-third from corporate contributors; the New Democrats received one-third of their funding from trade unions. The Bloc had rejected contributions from nonvoters until 2000 when it reversed this internal policy and began accepting corporate and trade union gifts.

Like their national party, Liberal candidates raised more funds from corporations than from individuals in 2000, though it should be noted that the corporate contributions made to most candidates came primarily from local businesses. A review of Elections Canada data for the 2000 election suggests that the candidates who raise significant

Table 7.1

Sources of party funds, 2000

	Bloc Québécois		Canadian Alliance		Liberal		New Democratic		Progressive Conservative	
	$	%	$	%	$	%	$	%	$	%
Individuals	1,663,967	74	11,954,957	61	6,966,801	35	5,752,150	64	2,778,118	49
Corporations	360,153	16	6,753,356	34	11,862,693	59	198,757	2	2,777,286	49
Trade unions	36,008	2	–	0	77,331	0.4	3,022,480	34	–	0
Total receipts from all sources	2,259,752		19,641,006		20,067,821		8,978,136		5,621,694	

Note: Proportions are similar for the nonelection year of 1999.
Source: Elections Canada 2000.

Table 7.2

Sources of candidate funds, 2000

	Bloc Québécois		Canadian Alliance		Liberal		New Democratic		Progressive Conservative	
	$	No.	$	No.	$	No.	$	No.	$	No.
Individuals	2,053,370	9,493	5,008,377	25,149	4,413,313	17,642	1,607,025	10,822	1,978,409	8,000
Corporations	433,733	922	2,354,608	4,572	5,173,777	8,299	493,567	366	1,030,661	2,516
Trade unions	25,625	21	3,650	3	136,062	103	847,666	910	5,600	5

Note: This table should be read for approximate proportions of corporate, union, and individual funds. In addition to direct contributions from individuals, unions, and corporations, many candidates are funded through party transfers and it is impossible to track the source of these funds.
Source: Elections Canada 2000.

amounts of funds from national corporate entities are primarily high-profile ministers and opposition party leaders.

The intent of corporate and trade union donors is impossible to discern. While some may be trying to curry favour with the government, others may be trying to avoid the negative repercussions of not contributing (particularly in cases where all the major competitors in a given industry contribute; see the number of banks making large contributions in Table 7.3). Some organizations may see it as a worthy investment in the public good. Nonetheless, at a minimum, large campaign contributions win the contributor valuable access to elected office holders. If for no other reason than good manners, elected politicians take the phone calls of those who have helped them with substantial contributions. In recent elections, a disproportionate number of these large contributors have been corporations and trade unions.

The availability of large corporate and trade union contributions also makes the parties less dependent on modest contributions from individuals. Consequently parties exert less effort to contact individual voters and win financial support from them. This has important implications beyond traditional campaign finance concerns. As discussed in Chapter 2, Canada's parties have few members, and turnout among potential voters is declining dramatically. Data from the 2000 Canada Election Study show a positive relationship between voter contact and voter turnout (Blais et al. 2002). Those contacted by a party are significantly more likely to vote. If parties were more dependent on voters for their finances, they might increase their efforts to contact voters and encourage them to become ongoing supporters of the party.

In recent years, there has been considerable public pressure on Parliament to take steps to minimize the role of corporations and trade unions in campaign financing. Canadians' view that their elected officials are unresponsive and out of touch with the concerns of average voters are given legitimacy by the extent of the parties' financial dependence on corporate and labour interests. In the wake of the 2000 campaign, many editorialists and public interest groups argued that the extreme reliance on corporate funding (especially by the governing

Table 7.3

Ten largest contributions to each of the five major parties, 2000

Party	Donor	Amount ($)
Liberal	Canadian Imperial Bank of Commerce	154,637
	Merrill Lynch Canada Inc.	124,853
	Bombardier Inc.	100,503
	The Bank of Nova Scotia	98,469
	Canadian National	93,148
	Royal Bank of Canada	90,618
	RBC Dominion Securities Inc.	84,002
	The Toronto Dominion Bank	77,171
	Toronto Dominion Securities Inc.	73,476
	Banque Nationale du Canada	72,705
Canadian Alliance	Eiram Development Corp	152,000
	Fraser, Milner, Casgrain	131,000
	The Bank of Nova Scotia	127,570
	Domgroup Ltd.	123,950
	Canadian Imperial Bank of Commerce	122,887
	Stanley Milner	106,100
	Bank of Montreal	103,640
	577710 Ontario Inc.	100,000
	George S. Petty Management Ltd.	100,000
	Royal Bank of Canada	94,986
Bloc Québécois	Parti Québécois	166,400
	TCA Trade Union	20,000
	Succession Robert Lauzière	17,067
	Samson, Bélair Deloitte & Touche	10,000
	Fédération des travailleurs et travailleuses du Québéc	8,425
	Impérial Tobacco Canada Ltée.	5,700
	Pierrette Venne	5,413
	Vidéotron Communications Inc.	5,055
	Succession Léo Bernier	5,000
	S.C.C. de l'Émergie de du Papier	5,000
New Democratic	Canadian Labour Congress	683,947
	CAW National Headquarters	452,177
	USWA National Headquarters	254,416
	UFCW National Headquarters	196,670
	CUPE National Headquarters	192,108
	USWA District 6	178,945
	CEP National Headquarters	139,261
	Canadian Machinist Political League	97,748
	Stuart McLeod	46,609
	Ontario Federation of Labour	44,883

......→

Party	Donor	Amount ($)
Progressive Conservative	Canadian Imperial Bank of Commerce	95,711
	Bank of Montreal	93,711
	Ted Rogers	90,000
	BCE Inc.	75,000
	Toronto Dominion Securities Inc.	63,711
	The Toronto Dominion Bank	56,025
	Canadian National Railways	49,725
	The Bank of Nova Scotia	46,490
	RBC Dominion Securities Inc.	44,498
	Imperial Tobacco Canada Ltd.	42,675

←···· Table 7.3

Source: Elections Canada 2000.

party) created at least the impression of a government beholden to corporate interests. Many advocated that the federal system follow the lead of the provinces of Quebec and Manitoba and restrict political contributions to eligible voters. The logic is that elections are to be decided by voters, and since we do not grant corporations or trade unions votes, we should not let them influence the electoral outcome by contributing large amounts of money to the parties. As illustrated in Table 7.3, almost all of the largest contributions to parties in the 2000 election cycle came from corporate and trade union interests. Of the fifty contributions listed, only six are from individuals.

The flood of corporate and trade union dollars into the parties' and candidates' coffers made them all vulnerable to charges that they are beholden to special interests. Not a session of Parliament went by without an opposition critic or a public interest group accusing a government of granting special treatment to its corporate contributors. Governments, with their hands in the corporate cookie jar, had no defence to these charges (other than arguing that the opposition parties have their hands as deep in corporate and union pockets as they do, an argument hardly likely to inspire voter confidence).

The principal argument advanced by those opposed to a prohibition on corporate and trade union contributions is that such a ban would starve candidates and parties of much-needed campaign funds. Many election campaign expenses relate to parties and candidates communicating with voters, something to be encouraged. Because most of this communication takes place via television, parties require substantial amounts of money to wage their campaigns. The donut retailer Tim Hortons spent an estimated $35 million on advertising in 2000 (Smith 2001). All our political parties combined spent about the same for their entire campaign efforts in the same year. Meanwhile, more than US$3,265 million was spent on the 2000 presidential and congressional elections in the United States (US Federal Elections Commission data). The point is that Canadian parties and candidates are not spending an inordinate amount of money. Reformers need to be careful not to create a system that leaves the parties and candidates without enough funds to wage vigorous election campaigns.

The parties have argued that if corporate and trade union contributions are banned, they will lose a substantial portion of their funding. This argument assumes, however, that the parties would not be able to replace these lost funds. Experience in Quebec, which has banned contributions to provincial parties from all but eligible voters since the late 1970s, indicates that parties are able to adapt to such rules and raise more funds from other sources. The Quebec Liberal Party was heavily reliant on corporate contributions prior to the changes to the province's election law. Louis Massicotte (1991) examined the Liberals' experience after the law changed and found that the party successfully switched its fundraising strategy. In almost no time it replaced the corporate funds with newfound support from individual contributors. Similarly, Massicotte found that, on a per capita basis, the revenues of Quebec provincial parties slightly exceed those of parties in the rest of Canada, where corporate and trade union contributions are allowed.

A similar development took place in Ontario. While the province does not prohibit corporate and union contributions, in 1975 it imposed limits of $8,000 on all contributions to parties and $1,500 on contributions to candidates. In response, the parties, which had been substantially dependent on large corporate and trade union contributions, broadened their fundraising appeals. As a result, the percentage of total receipts made up of corporate contributions to both the Conservative and Liberal parties decreased dramatically, as did the percentage of trade union receipts to the NDP. At the same time the number of individual contributions to the three parties rose by more than 400 percent in the ten years following the law change (Johnson 1991).

The recent experience in Manitoba, however, suggests that not all parties are able to adjust quickly to the prohibition of corporate and trade union contributions. The province's NDP government adopted these restrictions before the 2003 provincial election, and only the governing party appears to have significantly increased the amount of funds received from individuals. The opposition Conservative and Liberal parties have had substantially greater difficulty. Both parties saw a dramatic decline in their total receipts from the previous election and claimed that they were not able to raise sufficient funds to wage a competitive campaign. Both of these parties also drastically reduced their use of paid media. The result was a 2003 election campaign in which the opposition parties had few resources and were greatly handicapped in their ability to mount a vigorous challenge to the government.

Ontario and New Brunswick take an interesting approach by allowing corporations and trade unions to contribute to parties and candidates and capping these contributions at reasonably modest limits ($6,000 in New Brunswick). By limiting the size of contributions, this legislation makes the parties less likely to depend on a few large contributors, and encourages them to diversify their fundraising appeals. As the Ontario parties learned, there are only so many corporations and trade unions, and in order to obtain sufficient numbers of modest contributions they have to raise a significant amount of their funds from voters.

Prior to 2003 the federal system was deficient in this regard, as there were no limits on the amount that any eligible contributor could give. If a party so chose, and if a donor were willing, its entire campaign could be legally bankrolled by a single corporation or industry (and, remember, the source of the funds need not be disclosed until well after the election). Contribution limits help ensure that parties and candidates are not overly dependent on a few large contributors, and, as shown by the Ontario experience, tend to encourage parties and candidates to expand their efforts to receive modestly sized contributions from voters. While the vast majority of contributions received by parties and candidates are in amounts less than $1,000, Table 7.3 includes twenty contributions of at least $100,000.

Responding to these arguments, the federal Liberal government included a limit of $5,000 on contributions from individuals and what essentially amounts to a prohibition on corporate and trade union contributions in its 2003 reform legislation. The $5,000 limit should have little effect on party and candidate fundraising as very few contributions from individuals exceed this amount. On the other hand, the effect of the provisions relating to corporations and trade unions will be dramatic.

The principle of restricting financial participation in elections to voters has obvious democratic appeal. Nonetheless, the new federal legislation raises several concerns. The first is that it deprives the parties of much-needed funds. The legislation compensates by injecting massive amounts of new public money into the system (the implications of this are considered below). The second concern is that attempts to prohibit financial participation by corporations and trade unions in elections may not reduce their influence but rather divert funds out of the reach of the regulatory scheme and the transparency it ensures. Essentially, the worry is that corporations and unions may find ways to circumvent the law. Massicotte (2001) suggests that this has occurred in Quebec, identifying several ways in which these supposedly banned funds continue to make their way into the system. For example, corporations have been found to pay bonuses to their senior employees for the explicit purpose of having the employees contribute the funds to a favoured party. What is lost in this transaction is any public disclosure of the true source of the funds.

Uncertainty also remains at the federal level regarding the ability of Parliament to regulate spending by independent groups in campaigns. Parliament has passed legislation that severely limits such spending. However, this legislation is currently being challenged in the courts on the grounds that it violates provisions of the Charter of Rights and Freedoms. Should the courts strike down the legislation (as they have several similar earlier laws), corporations and trade unions would be free to spend as much as they like during election campaigns so long as they do not contribute the funds directly to candidates or parties. This would threaten the place of parties as the primary actors in our elections and have far-reaching implications for the health of parties as democratic institutions.

Essentially, the concern is that attempts to prohibit corporate and trade union financial participation in elections are similar to the "whack-a-mole" game found at carnivals and county fairs. The mole pops up in one place and the player whacks it down. But the mole doesn't go away; instead it randomly pops up somewhere else. This has been the experience in the United States, where repeated attempts to prohibit financial participation in federal elections by corporations and trade unions have routinely resulted in their finding new and creative ways to participate outside of the regulatory scheme. The provincial schemes that allow modest corporate and trade union financial participation within the regulatory framework may in the long run be more effective.

Equity and Accessibility

The values of equity and accessibility are complementary and can thus be examined together. These principles concern the ability of the major parties and their candidates to garner enough campaign funding to be financially competitive and to protect against one party or candidate wildly outspending its opponents.

These objectives are met through public financing and spending limitations. The purpose of public financing is usually stated as ensuring that all competitive candidates and parties have a minimum amount of funds to support their campaigns and helping lessen the pressure on candidates to raise funds from private sources. The purpose of spending limits is to prevent one party or candidate from spending large amounts of funds and thus drowning out the voices of their opponents. Essentially, these regulations attempt to narrow the range of the amounts spent by various players by forcing them between a floor (the amount of public financing they are eligible for) and a ceiling (the spending limitation imposed upon them). Establishing a floor level of funding enhances accessibility, and imposing a ceiling enhances equity.

The Canada Elections Act includes the following provisions:

* Candidates who receive at least 10 percent of the vote in a general election are eligible for public funds equal to 60 percent of their total campaign expenditures. These public funds are transmitted after the election campaign concludes.
* Parties are eligible for a yearly allowance equal to the number of votes received in the past election multiplied by $1.75 (paid quarterly), and for reimbursement of 50 percent of their election expenses provided they receive 2 percent of the popular vote.
* The public treasury also supports campaign spending through a tax credit scheme for political contributions. The amount of the credit begins at 75 percent for contributions up to $400, is reduced to 50 percent for the next $350, and to 33.3 percent for additional amounts to a maximum credit of $650.
* Parties are eligible for a limited amount of free radio and television broadcasting time.
* Candidates are limited to spending an amount determined by multiplying a factor adjusted for inflation by the number of voters in their riding (with some additional allowance made for large rural districts). In 2000, the average spending limit for candidates was $68,019.37.
* The spending limit for parties is determined by a formula based on the total number of voters in ridings where the party has endorsed a candidate. Parties endorsing candidates in all 301 ridings in 2000 were permitted to spend $12,710,074.11.

Public Financing

Election competition is a democratic necessity and as such is a public good. It is therefore appropriate for voters to pay a substantial portion of the costs from the public purse. The Canadian system succeeds at getting large amounts of public money to the parties and candidates and thus partially alleviating fundraising pressures. In 2000, parties received funding totalling slightly more than $7.5 million, and reimbursements to candidates totalled approximately $16 million. The total value of the tax credit for the year 2000 is estimated at more than $19 million (Canada Customs and Revenue Agency, Income Statistics, 2000 tax year).

In addition, an annual allowance came into effect in 2004, dramatically increasing the public financing of parties. Under the system in place from 1974 to 2003, parties received direct public financing only once per election cycle in an amount equal to 22.5 percent of their election expenses. The new legislation increased this amount to 50 percent in addition to the annual allowances. When introducing the new legislation to the House of Commons, Prime Minister Chrétien estimated that it would result in nine of every ten dollars spent by parties and candidates being taxpayer dollars. The government justified this massive infusion of public funding as necessary to offset the loss of corporate and trade union funds.

While some taxpayer support for campaigns and parties can be defended as a public investment in democracy, the extent of public money provided for in the new legislation is troubling. Under this system, parties are no longer dependent on raising funds from their supporters. Under the pre-2003 scheme, even with no restrictions on contribution size, the parties raised substantial funds in small contributions from individual voters. This required parties to communicate continuously with their supporters in order to maintain their support. The new system removes this incentive by dramatically increasing the parties' public entitlement and by basing the amount received on the number of votes won in the previous election. Essentially, the new system makes political parties wards of the state and diminishes the incentive to communicate with partisans between elections and involve them in party affairs.

The new system also heavily favours governing parties, as they are almost certain to have received more votes than any of the other parties in the previous election and thus are entitled to greater public financing in the run-up to the next election. New parties emerging between elections (as did the Reform Party and Bloc Québécois between 1988 and 1993) are not entitled to a quarterly allowance until after an election campaign in which they will be competing against established parties benefiting from substantial public grants.

The 2003 legislation reduced the vote threshold for eligibility for public financing for candidates from 15 to 10 percent, making these funds available to considerably more candidates. The number of major party candidates reaching the previous threshold decreased significantly in the last decade. As discussed in Chapter 6, with five credible parties, the federal vote is significantly more fragmented, making it more difficult for weaker candidates to reach the threshold. The percentage of candidates qualifying for direct public funding has decreased from 52 percent in 1974 to 47 percent in 1988 to 38 percent in 2000. Approximately 680 out of more than 1,800 candidates in 2000 qualified for the public funding. It is not only candidates of minor parties that are shut out of these funds. As shown in Table 7.4, most Liberal and Bloc candidates met the threshold, but four in ten Alliance candidates, seven in ten Conservatives, and eight in ten New Democrats did not qualify for direct public funds. Only two candidates who were not endorsed by one of the five major parties reached the 15 percent mark.

In recent elections, the Liberal Party, because of its electoral success, has benefited far more than any other party from the direct public financing scheme. The discrepancy in the number of candidates receiving public funding among the major parties raises issues of equity. The 2003 reforms lowering the threshold to 10 percent will help address this somewhat. If the lower threshold had been in place for the 2000 election, 121 additional candidates would have qualified for public funding and the majority of these would have come from the

Table 7.4

Candidates meeting the 15 percent threshold for public financing in 2000, by party and province

	Liberal	CA	BQ	NDP	PC	Total seats
Territories	3/3	2/2	–	3/3	0/3	3
British Columbia	33/34	33/34	–	7/34	0/34	34
Alberta	18/26	26/26	–	1/25	5/26	26
Saskatchewan	10/14	14/14	–	14/14	0/11	14
Manitoba	14/14	11/14	–	8/14	4/14	14
Ontario	103/103	86/103	–	13/103	47/100	103
Quebec	75/75	3/73	69/75	0/72	2/71	75
New Brunswick	10/10	6/10	–	1/10	9/10	10
Nova Scotia	11/11	1/11	–	7/11	10/11	11
Prince Edward Island	4/4	0/4	–	1/4	4/4	4
Newfoundland	7/7	0/7	–	2/7	6/7	7
Total	288/301	182/298	69/75	57/298	87/291	301

opposition parties. The Conservatives would have benefited the most with an additional fifty-five candidates qualifying, followed by twenty-nine New Democrats, twenty-five Alliance candidates, ten Liberals, and one Bloc candidate. One additional unaffiliated candidate would have qualified.

The existence of a threshold is reasonable to ensure that taxpayer funds are spent only on serious candidates and not available to everyone who decides to list their name on the ballot. However, one wonders why the threshold for parties to be eligible for public funding is set at 2 percent of the vote, while candidates are required to meet a bar set 500 percent higher. Even with the lower 10 percent threshold, Liberal and Bloc candidates would have benefited far more than any of their opponents. In 2000, 99 percent of Liberal candidates received 10 percent or more of the vote, compared with 97 percent of Bloc candidates, 69 percent of Alliance candidates, 49 percent of Conservatives, and 29 percent of New Democrats.

The advantage is even greater than these numbers indicate. Virtually all Liberal candidates can be quite certain that they will qualify for the public rebate and can plan their campaign budgets accordingly. Most candidates in the other parties, including many of those who ultimately receive 10 percent of the vote, cannot be so certain. Only 1 percent of Bloc and 7 percent of Liberal candidates who received public funding won between 15 and 20 percent of the vote in 2000, compared with 17 percent of Alliance candidates, 30 percent of New Democrats, and 47 percent of Tories. This means that of the eighty-seven Tories who received public funding, forty-one of them barely qualified and thus were probably uncertain about their prospects of receiving any direct public funds. Because the funds are only made available after the campaign, and because many of these opposition candidates cannot count on qualifying for them, it is unclear that the public funds assist them in mounting a credible, competitive campaign.

Data from the 2000 election show that candidates winning 20 percent or more of the vote spent considerably more than did their colleagues who received between 15 and 20 percent. Alliance candidates receiving more than 20 percent spent an average of $49,267, while candidates falling in the 15 to 20 percent range spent an average of $33,701. The trend is similar in each of the parties. The differences result from many factors, including parties targeting their efforts on those seats they think they might win, but they may also reflect the unwillingness of candidates in the opposition parties to count prematurely on receiving a public rebate.

By not providing funding to candidates of major parties that fall short of the threshold, the system reinforces the strong regional character of electoral competition in Canada. As discussed in Chapter 6, the workings of the first-past-the-post electoral system require all parties to concentrate their resources on ridings where they have a reasonable chance of winning a plurality of the vote. Accordingly, candidates can expect little help from their national campaigns if they are running in a province or region where support for their party is weak. By also denying these candidates public funding, the electoral system makes it very difficult for them to mount anything more than a token effort. For example, the national Progressive Conservative Party spent little in British Columbia and Quebec in the 2000 campaign, realizing that it had little chance of electing members from these provinces. Conservative candidates in these provinces, with little help from the national office, also knew they were not likely to reach the 15 percent threshold and thus could not expect the public subsidy. As a result many local Conservative campaigns in these provinces were skeletal operations with few resources to undertake anything approaching a real electoral effort. Only one in five of the party's Quebec candidates and less than half of its candidates in British Columbia spent more than $5,000 (Elections Canada 2000).

Lowering the threshold to 10 percent helps to address this regional disparity somewhat. If the 10 percent rule had been in place in 2000, Liberals would have benefited on the Prairies; Conservatives in Ontario, Alberta, and British Columbia; New Democrats in Atlantic Canada, Ontario, and British Columbia; and Alliance candidates in Atlantic Canada, Quebec, and Ontario. In other words all of the parties would have seen a significant increase in the number of their candidates receiving public funding in areas of the country where they are electorally weak. Lowering the threshold further would have an even greater levelling effect.

Because the public financing to candidates is made available only after the election, the question of how the money is spent must be considered. Many incumbents and candidates in safe ridings have no difficulty during the campaign raising the full amount they are allowed to spend and then receive public funds afterward that are not needed to pay debts from the past campaign. Two things routinely happen to these funds. First, the national parties often require their candidates to forfeit a portion of the funds (as much as 50 percent) to the party's headquarters. This significant portion of the public financing therefore never reaches its intended recipient, the local candidate. The second outcome, primarily in the case of incumbents, is that the funds that do reach the candidate are not needed for the election in which they are given, and so are deposited into the local riding association's bank accounts. Many long-term incumbents have built up substantial balances in their local association's bank accounts.

Table 7.5

Election expenses, spending limits, and treasury reimbursements of major parties, 2000

	Election expenses ($)	Authorized limit ($)	Percentage of limit spent (%)	Reimbursement ($)
BQ	1,968,693	3,383,175	59	404,402
CA	9,669,648	12,638,257	77	2,167,502
Liberal	12,525,174	12,710,074	99	2,809,219
NDP	6,334,585	12,584,911	50	1,423,516
PC	3,983,301	12,352,405	32	875,701

Source: Elections Canada data , <www.elections.ca>.

SPENDING LIMITS

While public financing aims at setting a floor for candidate and party spending, limits set a ceiling beyond which they cannot spend. Table 7.5 displays the actual election expenses of the major parties in the 2000 election, their spending limits, and the amounts reimbursed from the public treasury. What is clear from this table is that only the Liberals were constrained by the spending cap as none of the others spent as much as 80 percent of their allowable limits.

Prior to the 2003 reform legislation, many candidate and party expenses were not included in the definition of "election expenses" used by Elections Canada and thus were exempt from these spending limits. These included big-ticket items such as public opinion polling and all campaign expenses incurred before the official start of the campaign. The result was that parties could spend considerably more on their campaign efforts than their reported election expenses indicate. The 2003 reforms include polling expenses within the limits; however, as parties increasingly engage in television and radio advertising campaigns in the weeks before the election is called, a significant loophole remains.

One way to capture some of the campaign spending by parties that is not included in their reported election expenses is to examine their annual fiscal returns. In these reports parties list their annual spending not including any "election expenses." As illustrated in Table 7.6, the amount spent by the Alliance and Liberals in 2000 was dramatically higher than that spent in nonelection years. Some of the Alliance spending may be related to the party's 2000 leadership contest, but the Liberal increase seems wholly related to the 2000 election (particularly considering that a similar spike in Liberal spending occurred in 1997). A more accurate picture of Liberal Party spending on the 2000 election may be reached by adding the party's reported election expenses of $12.5 million to the $7 million increase in annual spending in 2000 for a total of almost $20 million. This amount is far in excess of the prescribed limit and far more than that spent by any of its opponents. The Liberal Party is in no way violating the law in this regard. Rather, as the governing party it has the greatest access to private money, and the exceptions in the regulatory definition of "election expenses" allow parties to spend virtually as much as they can raise.

Individual candidates were limited to spending approximately $68,000 in 2000. Like the party limits this amount is adjusted annually to reflect inflation and was increased modestly in the 2003 legislation from 62 cents to 70 cents per elector. This relatively low limit ensures that no local candidate will spend lavishly on her campaign and thus lessens the fundraising pressures on all candidates. These low limits on candidate spending also ensure that parties will be the principal communicators during campaigns. An individual candidate

Table 7.6

Annual party nonelection spending by fiscal year, 1996-2000

	1996 ($)	1997 ($)	1998 ($)	1999 ($)	2000 ($)
BQ	1,289,301	3,226,722	711,239	1,051,512	1,884,922
Reform/Alliance	7,220,404	6,215,979	6,156,340	6,246,471	15,304,605
Liberal	13,192,806	20,022,369	12,790,570	12,605,399	19,569,874
PC	6,590,012	11,095,736	5,102,034	5,137,926	4,878,472

Note: NDP reports include funds spent on provincial party organization and thus do not provide a clear picture of spending by the federal party.
Source: Elections Canada data, <www.elections.ca>.

is not able to spend enough to separate herself from the message communicated by her party. This helps to preserve the primary place of parties in the Canadian electoral system.

Party Leadership and Nomination Contests

Prior to the 2003 reforms, two significant aspects of Canadian electoral competition were left completely unregulated: candidate nomination campaigns and party leadership selection contests. There were no spending limits, no contribution prohibitions or limitations, and no disclosure requirements. Parties argued, and Parliament through its inaction agreed, that these were internal party contests and thus should be left to the parties to operate and regulate. This logic is faulty in both contexts. Neither leadership nor nomination contests are private party affairs and parties have not done a satisfactory job of regulating the financing of either. The remainder of this section considers leadership selection, but most of the argument here is also applicable to candidate nomination contests.

If Canadians are concerned with accessibility in their politics and protecting against undue influence by moneyed interests, then we must concern ourselves with the electoral contests that choose party leaders. Attempting to prevent quid pro quo arrangements between candidates and large financial contributors by regulating general elections may well be too late. When a potential prime minister most needs financial support is during a leadership contest. These are often hotly contested elections that cost millions of dollars. From the perspective of a contributor this is an ideal time to support a candidate. In fact, many large contributors decide to hedge their bets and bankroll all those with a chance of winning. For example, more than two dozen contributors gave thousands of dollars each to more than one of the candidates in the 1990 Liberal contest (Cross 1992, 44-5).

Faced with public consternation, and concern from the ranks of their own activists, that large amounts of unregulated funds are being spent in leadership contests, parties began to establish rules aimed at providing the appearance of self-regulation. These efforts usually amounted to little more than window dressing. Even when parties did establish spending limits and disclosure requirements, candidates routinely spent far beyond the established limits and failed to disclose all of their contributors without facing any penalty. No party has ever sanctioned its leader for failing to comply with its internal spending and reporting rules.

We do not know how much candidates spend on leadership races, because they have been under no legal requirement to disclose their expenditures. Parties release partial information, and occasionally campaign operatives disclose some information, which allows an estimation of the costs. Sometimes parties set limits and sometimes not. For example, the Canadian Alliance decided not to impose any limit on the amount candidates in its 2000 leadership contest could spend. The Liberal Party set a limit of $1.7 million per candidate for its 1990 contest and increased this to $4 million for its 2003 race. Among expenditures exempted from these limits, however, were all costs incurred prior to the official launch of the leadership campaign. In both contests the principal candidates had been campaigning for many months (in Chrétien's and Martin's cases for years) prior to the contests, with none of the expenses for these preparatory activities counting against the spending limit. In fact, the campaigns of the leading candidates in the 1990 contest admitted to spending more than 150 percent of the limit. Liberal cabinet member Lloyd Axworthy summed up the effectiveness of the party regulations: "If they can raise it they can spend it, the sky's the limit" (Thompson 1990).

In the 1993 Conservative contest, the party set a limit of $900,000. As in the earlier Liberal contest many campaign expenses were exempt, allowing candidate Jean Charest to spend two and a half times the limit without violating the party's rules. Winning candidate Kim Campbell reportedly spent approximately $3 million. Not surprisingly, the party took no action against either campaign. The inability of parties to police their own contests was equally evident in 1976 when Brian Mulroney refused to comply with the Progressive Conservative

Party's disclosure requirements. Not only was he not sanctioned, but he went on to win the next Conservative leadership contest in 1983.

A lack of meaningful spending limitations has prevented potentially competitive candidates from entering these contests. Lloyd Axworthy's concern that he could not raise the millions of dollars to compete with Chrétien and Martin in 1990 was decisive in his not entering the race. Criticizing the party's financing rules, Axworthy contended, "The power of big money should not be the dominant factor in determining the outcome of any political decision the party makes" (Leadership rules 1989). Long-time Conservative cabinet member Perrin Beatty gave similar reasons for avoiding his party's 1993 contest.

When parties do require disclosure reports, they are often incomplete and largely indecipherable. The 1990 Liberal contest provides a good example of this. While the party released lists of those who received tax receipts for giving more than $100 to candidates, the lists include only a small portion of total receipts and often do not provide adequate identifying information. Chrétien's list totals approximately $875,000, or one-third of his claimed total expenditures. Martin's disclosed total of about $390,000 represents only one-seventh of his claimed spending (Liberal Party of Canada 1990). It is highly unlikely that either candidate raised the remainder of their funds (over $2 million each) in contributions of less than $100. Moreover, the disclosure information released by the party includes only the name of the contributor and the amount contributed. No further identifying information such as locale is provided, and the lists include many unidentifiable numbered corporations. In the 2003 Liberal contest, Prime Minister Chrétien insisted that any cabinet ministers seeking the leadership fully disclose their campaign finances. But the leading candidate, Paul Martin, was not subject to these rules as he left cabinet prior to the official start of the campaign.

The parties themselves have little confidence in their ability to effectively regulate the financing of these contests. This was made evident by Jan Dymond, co-chair of the Conservatives' 1998 leadership selection committee. In announcing the rules that would govern the contest, she said, "We're trying to structure a system that doesn't encourage people to hide expenditures and donations. We'll see if we're successful. I think there was a feeling candidates would want to be able to offer some people confidentiality on donations. And, frankly, if we were going to publish them all then the leadership campaigns simply wouldn't tell us about the donations" (Toulin 1998).

Parliament responded to some of the above concerns by bringing candidate nomination and leadership selection contests within the campaign finance regulatory framework. The 2003 legislation includes the following provisions:

* Nomination and leadership candidates are subject to financial disclosure requirements.
* Nomination candidates are limited to spending an amount equal to 20 percent of the amount a general election candidate is eligible to spend in the riding.
* Nomination and leadership candidates are subject to the same contribution source and size limitations as are general election candidates.

These new regulations mark a significant step forward. They recognize that leadership and nomination contests are important parts of the electoral process that must be included in attempts to ensure probity, equity, accessibility, and transparency. The regulations pertaining to leadership contests are particularly noteworthy, as they include a requirement for pre-election disclosure. Candidates are required to file financial disclosure reports four weeks prior to the vote and then weekly thereafter. The limit on nomination spending (of approximately $15,000) will be a real impediment only in the most hotly contested ridings. Most candidates report spending far less than this on their nomination campaigns. Nonetheless, women and visible minority candidates have complained that in the most competitive ridings, where massive recruitment drives are common in nomination contests, they have difficulty raising sufficient funds to be competitive. Given the paucity of female and minority MPs, regulations that increase their competitiveness in nomination contests should be viewed positively.

The new legislation falls short in not imposing a limit on leadership campaign spending. Candidates in the major parties spend millions of dollars in these races, which surely makes it difficult – if not impossible – for certain classes of candidates to compete. It is hard to understand why limits are needed for general election and nomination campaigns but not for these extremely important contests.

Financing Democracy

Ultimately, we concern ourselves with questions relating to campaign financing because we desire an electoral system that fosters the central democratic values of participation, responsiveness, and inclusiveness. These values argue for a regulatory framework that keeps political candidacy accessible to all, that encourages parties to receive their financial support through modest contributions from many voters, and that discourages financial dependency on corporations, trade unions, and other special interests. The newly adopted Canadian regulatory system receives a mixed report card on these criteria.

The system is participatory and inclusive in that through the use of reasonable spending limits, nomination and general election candidates need not be personally wealthy nor able to raise substantial amounts of money in order to compete. Nor need they worry that they will be vastly outspent during the general election campaign. The provision of partial public financing to candidates also helps those who might not be able to raise the required funds. The system could be improved by providing the direct public funds prior to the election and by limiting spending in party leadership contests.

The increased reliance of the parties on public funds raises important issues of responsiveness. Parties are meant to be instruments for citizens to influence and check their government. If parties are almost wholly funded by the state, their capacity to serve this function is brought into question. Similarly, given the already weak nature of parties as membership organizations, any reforms that weaken incentives for them to continuously solicit voter support are suspect.

Chapter 7

Party Financing

Disclosure

Strengths
- The public is provided with information on all contributions in excess of $200 to parties and candidates.

Weaknesses
- All disclosure of contributions, with the exception of party leadership contests, occurs after the election.

Limitations on Contributions

Strengths
- Contributions are prohibited from foreign nationals, corporations, and trade unions.
- There are limitations on the size of individual contributions to parties and candidates.

Weaknesses
- The prohibition on corporate and trade union contributions may not be enforceable and may result in less transparency.

Public Financing

Strengths
- Substantial amounts of public funds are provided to candidates and parties.
- Public financing lessens pressure on parties and candidates to raise funds from private sources.
- All parties receive some free television and radio exposure.

Weaknesses
- The funding threshold (the percentage of votes a candidate must receive) is set too high, denying many candidates access to direct public funds.
- Public money is available to candidates only after the election, minimizing its usefulness.
- The amount of public funds received is based on votes won in the past election, which greatly benefits the governing party.
- New legislation provides too much public money to parties, removing an important incentive for them to continually seek voter support between election campaigns.

Spending Limits

Strengths
- Candidates are limited to spending moderate amounts, allowing most serious candidates to be financially competitive.

Weaknesses
- Limits exclude all party spending outside the election period and thus allow wealthy parties to spend considerably more than the set limit.

- There are no limits on spending in party leadership contests.

FOUR PROPOSALS FOR PARTY REFORM 8

Canadian voters are correct in their belief that political parties are crucial institutions in Canadian democracy. In a large and complex society, parties unite Canadians with one another and with their institutions of democratic governance. It is not surprising that at the end of the twentieth century when Canadians expressed general dissatisfaction with the state of their politics, this sentiment was accompanied by a substantial decline in voters' confidence in their parties. Nor was this loss of confidence misplaced: to a significant degree, parties are responsible for what voters are most dissatisfied with in their politics. The evidence is clear that Canadians find their politics overly elite dominated, insufficiently responsive to their views, and lacking in opportunities for them to influence policy outcomes. As the democratic institutions meant to provide participatory opportunity for voters, and to link them to central decision-making bodies, parties must shoulder a significant share of the responsibility for this voter discontent.

One of the objectives of the Democratic Audit project is to advance potential reforms. In this concluding chapter, the Audit benchmarks of participation, inclusiveness, and responsiveness are applied to the performance of the parties in each of the areas examined in earlier chapters to create a set of reform proposals. As established in Chapter 1, this emphasis on how the parties can do better should not be read as a complete indictment of our parties. As we have seen in each chapter, there are many things that the parties are doing well.

This chapter focuses on four sets of reforms that may enable parties to become more participatory, inclusive, and responsive while respecting the brokerage practices of the traditional parties. Not everyone will agree with these proposals. Nonetheless, the hope is that they will spark discussion about how best to adapt our parties to the changing democratic expectations of Canadians at the outset of the twenty-first century. The suggested reforms are:

- opening up the candidate nomination and leadership selection processes to include non-party members
- enriching the value and attraction of party membership by enhancing the role of grassroots members in policy study and development
- further reforming the campaign finance system to make parties less dependent on the public purse, to limit the spending of leadership candidates, to provide ongoing public financing for party policy institutions, to provide candidates with pre-election public financing, and to require pre-election disclosure of campaign receipts
- considering reform of the electoral system to include some method of proportional representation, so that parties are encouraged to campaign vigorously in all parts of the country and so the campaign efforts of their local volunteers are no longer essentially futile in many constituencies.

In terms of participation, the first observation is that few Canadians choose to belong to the parties and even fewer choose to be participants on an ongoing basis. Most Canadians choose among parties when they vote but do not choose to become active supporters of any party. It is not that Canadians are universally disinterested in politics and prefer to spend their time doing other things (though certainly many do!). The evidence is strong that many Canadians remain interested in politics and believe parties are crucial players in the political process. Equally, however, they reject the way parties are conducting their affairs and increasingly prefer to join interest groups or to participate in new social movements. As the authors of the *Absent mandate* series suggest, "They are interested and they want to be involved, yet they feel that they do not have access to the political process and that politicians and government are neither sufficiently responsive nor reliable" (Clarke et al. 1996, 181-2).

The parties do draw substantial numbers of voters to two of their activities: candidate nomination and leadership selection. Even though parties do not make participation in these events particularly easy, in any election cycle hundreds of thousands of Canadians participate in them. Voters join parties for nomination and leadership campaigns for two reasons. First, they are asked. The parties do not regularly engage in extensive membership mobilization activity. However, during nomination and leadership contests, partisans of the various contenders traditionally recruit new members to support their favoured candidates. Second, members play a consequential role in leadership and candidate selection contests. Members realize some return on their participation, because their preferences, unmediated by elites, normally determine the outcomes of these contests.

In Chapters 4 and 5, I argued that while participation in parties during these contests is more robust than during other periods, relatively few Canadians are involved, including only a small percentage of each party's own partisans. The principal reason suggested for this lack of widespread participation is that both of these contests are perceived (by the parties, the state, and voters) as private events of political parties. They are members-only affairs, and the rules governing the contests are determined, for the most part, solely by the parties. Through imposition of rules such as voting fees and early membership cut-off dates, and, at least in the case of nominations, use of polling locations not easily accessible to all voters, the parties themselves discourage their casual partisans from participating. Rather, they favour participation by members of cohesive groups who are the subject of well-organized mobilization efforts by the candidates and their supporters. Many loyal electoral supporters of a party, who generally do not regularly purchase a party membership, may not even know the contest is taking place in time to register to participate.

More Open Nomination and Leadership Selection

The first reform possibility is that candidate nomination and leadership selection processes be opened up to all interested voters and that voting methods be more similar to those used during general elections. In candidate nomination, this may involve the state operating nomination voting for all registered parties on a single day shortly after the campaign writ is issued. Parties should be allowed to set their own rules for candidacy, and to continue forming local search committees to encourage participation from members of underrepresented groups. However, voting in the nomination contest should be open to all voters who wish to participate. Voting in a manner similar to a general election, on a common date, and using the permanent voters list, would allow Canadians to anticipate when the elections will be held and to participate without having to travel long distances to a single site in their riding, without having to register well in advance of the event, without having to pay a voting fee, and without having to commit several evening or weekend hours to voting. Rather, interested partisans would be able to drop into their local voting place and cast their ballot within minutes. Poll clerks would have ballots available for each registered party (containing the candidate names forwarded by the parties) and voters would ask for the ballot of the party of their choice.

Likely objections to such a system include that it creates the possibility for mischief making by nonsupporters of a party, that it diminishes the value of party membership, that it takes much-needed funds out of the parties' coffers, and that it reduces the discretion of central party operatives in candidate nomination. Each of these concerns is addressed in turn below.

Essentially, parties allow anyone to participate in nomination and leadership contests today, even some who are not eligible to vote in general elections. Many of those participating in these contests are not long-term members of the party, but rather are mobilized to membership in support of a particular candidate. The opportunity for a party outsider to win a nomination or leadership with the support of many who have never before belonged to the party already exists in the present system. And most parties' rules currently allow voters to participate in the nomination contests of more than one party in the same election cycle. This would not be allowed in the proposed system. Limiting voters to participation in a single nomination contest would encourage those who participate to vote in the nomination contest they are most interested in. Motivating large numbers of people to turn out to vote for the sole purpose of mischief making is unlikely. There is no evidence of this happening in open leadership contests (like the Alberta Conservative contest that chose Ralph Klein and was essentially open to all Albertans), or in US states with open primary elections.

Given that one of the principal benefits of party membership is the privilege of voting in leadership and nomination campaigns, parties may well argue that allowing nonmembers this privilege would remove an important incentive to membership. The weakness in this argument is that it assumes that parties somehow benefit from the large number of members attracted to membership because of these contests. The evidence presented in Chapter 2 is unequivocal that most of those mobilized into membership for these contests do not retain their memberships afterwards. They do not become ongoing, active members of the parties' local constituency associations. The few members who belong to parties in interelection periods do so for other reasons, not because they wish to participate in one of these contests. It is difficult to see how parties would lose many of their long-term members because of such reform. Candidates use nomination and leadership contests as a way to build a team of volunteers to manage their subsequent general election campaign. The proposed reform would not deprive candidates and parties of this opportunity, as they would still have to organize a nomination or leadership campaign effort to attract their supporters to the polls.

The only lasting benefit parties realize from these membership mobilization efforts is the substantial swelling of their bank accounts from payment of membership fees. This is a significant concern. Parties need funds to mount their subsequent election campaigns. This concern can be addressed in two possible ways. The first is more substantial and ongoing public financing for the parties. The significant increase in public funding included in the 2003 reforms to the Canada Elections Act should more than replace the need for parties to raise funds through what essentially amounts to a poll tax. Second, and perhaps more importantly for the long-term health of the parties, they would be encouraged to offer some alternative value in party membership, so that voters might still be enticed to join and participate in party activities. An increase in grassroots participation in policy development, as discussed below, may provide this incentive. The evidence recounted in Chapters 2 and 3 suggests that current members are dissatisfied with the opportunities afforded them in this regard and that voters generally do not see membership in parties as an effective way to influence policy. Changing this perception, admittedly not an easy task, could encourage more voters to join parties on an ongoing basis. Without the funds brought in through nomination and leadership contest poll taxes, parties would be encouraged to reform themselves to attract members (and their dollars) through other means.

Limiting voting to those eligible to vote in general elections would be one of the costs of the proposed reform. This would affect the participation of noncitizens and those too young to vote (who are currently permitted to participate in some, but not all, parties). This cost does not appear overly great. As discussed in Chapter 2, noncitizens and youth mobilized for participation into nomination contests do not tend to maintain their involvement with parties after the contest. Participation by some of these voters is also highly contentious, with many party activists arguing that new immigrants are not casting deliberative ballots but rather are doing what they are asked to do by the leaders of their ethnic communities.

The current candidate nomination system allows central parties substantial control over the nomination process. As discussed in

Chapter 4, authority over candidate nomination normally lies with local associations, but central parties have intervened to appoint candidates, to prevent would-be candidates from running, and to encourage the nominations of women and visible minorities. The proposed system would not necessarily diminish the parties' prerogative in this regard, as they would be charged with forwarding the names of nomination candidates in each riding (and perhaps the actual ballots) to Elections Canada. This would permit parties to continue to deny candidacy to individuals they thought unsuitable and to maintain requirements such as the Alliance's provision that candidates agree with its overarching ideology. Undoubtedly, the increased public scrutiny that this type of reform would bring to the nomination process would make it more difficult for a party to unilaterally appoint a candidate.

In the case of leadership selection, the 1992 Alberta Conservative contest offers a template of an accessible and participatory process. From a participatory (and inclusiveness) perspective, the only drawback to this contest was the $5 voting fee. Otherwise, all interested Albertans could easily participate whether or not they had ever belonged to the party prior to voting in the contest. This election was similar to an open primary in the United States and achieved a similar participation rate, far greater than the Canadian norm. Considering that the person elected in many leadership contests automatically becomes premier or prime minister, it is difficult to justify restricting participation to members of one political party.

As discussed in Chapter 5, some parties are concerned about the potential loss of the collective decision-making opportunity provided by the leadership convention. This is an important concern for those parties engaged in the Canadian brokerage tradition. The method first used by the Ontario Liberals, and subsequently by both the federal Conservatives and Liberals, suggests a process that unites the participatory benefits of direct election with the accommodative opportunities of the convention. Recognizing this, any legislation relating to leadership selection should require that all voters be able to participate in the first instance by casting a direct ballot for their preferred leadership candidate, at no financial cost, and in a manner and place similar to general election voting. How these votes are then translated into the choice of a leader could be left to the discretion of the parties. Some might choose to count them by riding, giving equal weight to each constituency, some might prefer to guarantee a certain percentage of the votes to a particular class of members, and others to have the direct vote choose, on a proportionate basis, delegates to a leadership convention. The important points are that all voters are provided with the opportunity to vote directly for their preferred candidate and that parties are left with some discretion as to the kind of process that best reflects their democratic values.

More Grassroots Policy Development

In terms of responsiveness, the greatest challenge for the parties is to find a way for their grassroots activists to participate meaningfully, through the parties, in policy study and development. Party members are overwhelmingly dissatisfied with the role they play in policy development, and nonmembers suggest that they do not see participation in parties as a way to influence public policy. These attitudes contribute to the widely held perception that elected officials are out of touch with voters.

Parties face a tricky dilemma in this area. While turning policy development over to their members would probably increase their membership numbers (particularly for potential governing parties), this would not make them more responsive to the electorate at large. As well, the brokerage parties are charged not simply with responding to majority preferences but with accommodating divergent interests and fashioning a national interest which may not reflect majority opinion. The challenge is to permit significant involvement by the parties' activists while reserving the final say for the legislative caucus. Caucus decision making must be influenced by the actions of the grassroots members or the incentive to participate will disappear.

In Chapter 3, I argued that parties can enhance their capacity for policy development through the creation of ongoing, party-run policy foundations. Unlike parties in many European countries, most Canadian parties have not set up policy foundations, nor have they developed close ties with independent policy groups. The result is that parties have virtually no capacity for ongoing policy study and development. While party members report that they spend little or no time on policy development, an overwhelming majority of them suggest that they would like to do so.

Party policy foundations would allow party members to study policy issues, to debate alternatives, and to present their legislative caucuses with alternative policy approaches. Through these foundations, parties can increase representation in policy study to include groups (regional, sociodemographic, ideological) not represented in their legislative caucuses. This would be particularly beneficial for brokerage parties finding themselves without representation from significant segments of society in their elected caucuses.

Some parties have had short-term, vibrant policy processes while in opposition, but these have never lasted long nor been sustained while in government. The result is that voters interested in policy study are shunning the parties for other organizations such as interest groups. The creation of policy institutions with a meaningful role for party members would provide incentive for those voters interested in public policy to participate in the parties.

Parties have in the past complained that they simply do not have the necessary resources to maintain policy organizations between elections. But the newly adopted annual allowances of taxpayer funds provide the parties with a windfall of new resources. The parties may simply use these funds to replace those lost as a result of the prohibition on corporate and trade union contributions, or they may replace the lost funds through a re-energized effort at the grassroots level (as many provincial parties have done) and use some of the new public funding for other purposes. Parliament would have been wise to direct a significant portion of the annual allowance, in nonelection years, toward support of party policy foundations. Such a provision would ensure that some of the taxpayers' dollars provided to parties are used for the purpose of engaging voters in the policy study and development process. A provision requiring that parties establish policy foundations in order to receive the new public funding, and directing a sizeable portion of the annual allowances to these foundations, would be a worthwhile reform.

More Campaign Finance Reform

Reform of the campaign financing system is an important part of addressing voters' concerns relating to responsiveness and inclusiveness of the parties. The parties' reliance in recent election cycles on contributions from corporations and trade unions can only fuel voters' belief that the parties are overly responsive to these special interests. The 2003 legislation, in essentially prohibiting parties from receiving these funds, was a step in the right direction. While a prohibition may be difficult to enforce and, as I argued in Chapter 7, broadening the $5,000 limit imposed on contributions from voters to include unions and corporations might have been a better approach, the reforms adopted are an improvement over what preceded them.

The accompanying dramatic increase in public funding, however, without any requirement that some of the additional funds be used to support activities such as engaging voters in policy discussion, is not a step forward. Parties should be encouraged to raise a significant portion of their funds in small amounts from large numbers of voters. Parties must communicate with potential donors on an ongoing basis and be responsive to their concerns, and forcing parties to view voters as their primary donors would thus increase their communication with and responsiveness to the electorate. This is not accomplished by replacing corporate and trade union contributions dollar-for-dollar with taxpayer funds. As discussed in Chapter 7, the experiences at the provincial level suggest that parties are able to raise more of their funds from individuals when access to corporate, labour, and taxpayer dollars is limited. While the parties are highly unlikely to roll back the additional public funding they've just awarded themselves, Parliament should consider amending the 2003 legislation to redirect a portion of the taxpayers' subvention to support the development of party policy foundations. This, coupled with the ban on corporate and union contributions, would force the parties to make up any shortfall through contributions from voters.

The provision of public funding to candidates increases accessibility to public office both by decreasing the need to raise private funds and by providing a basic amount of financing for all serious candidates. The effectiveness of the current subsidy for candidates is minimized because the threshold for qualifying for public funding remains too high and because the money is made available only after the election. Eliminating, or dramatically lowering, the threshold and providing the funds before the election, when they are needed, would ensure that all candidates of the major parties are able to wage strong campaigns in all parts of the country. Reform legislation might provide that candidates representing parties that won 5 percent of the vote in a riding in the previous election would receive the public subvention (or a significant portion of it) at the outset of the campaign. Candidates of new parties without a track record in the riding could continue to be reimbursed retroactively. This reform would mostly benefit candidates running in areas of the country where their party is electorally weak and where few resources are expended by the central campaign. Pre-election public funding would assist these candidates to wage more vigorous campaigns and would decrease the degree of regionalism currently characterizing Canadian elections.

Regulating (and capping) the spending of candidates in leadership and nomination campaigns makes these contests accessible to more potential candidates. The new legislation imposes a cap on nomination spending, but not for leadership candidates. The need to restrict the amount spent on leadership campaigns is supported by evidence that candidates regularly use large war chests to discourage others from challenging them (for example, Conservative Kim Campbell in 1993 and Liberal Paul Martin in 2003). In 1991, the Royal Commission on Electoral Reform and Party Financing recommended a limit equal to 15 percent of the parties' spending limit in the prior election. For national parties this would currently equal about $2 million. Parties would still be able to set lower limits if they so chose. Adopting the commission's recommendation would protect against some of the excessive spending seen in recent contests by setting an outside limit.

Spending limits do not address the problem faced by many other candidates, women in particular, who do not have access to the traditional sources of campaign financing and thus find it extremely difficult to raise the funds necessary to wage a nomination or leadership campaign. In most nomination contests, the vast majority of candidates are not spending in excess of the new limit of $15,000 (see, for example, Carty and Erickson 1991). The real challenge is to create a system that provides every legitimate candidate with access to sufficient funding to allow them to run a competitive campaign. The extension of the tax credit provision to include contributions to candidates in party nomination and leadership contests will assist candidates in raising funds. A system providing some modest, direct public financing, perhaps through matching funds, would further help nomination and leadership candidates in getting a campaign off the ground. The method used in US presidential primary contests provides a useful model. In this system, candidates have the first $250 of contributions from individuals matched by the public treasury. Such a system has the advantage of ensuring that only those candidates with some public support, and those actively seeking modest contributions from voters, benefit from taxpayers' funds.

There is no justification for permitting leadership and nomination candidates not to disclose the sources of their campaign funds. Concern about whom elected officials are responsive to requires that interested voters have full knowledge of whom the candidates and parties are raising their campaign funds from. This is no less true of nomination and leadership campaigns than of general elections. The new requirement that these candidates file public returns is a positive step. Similarly, as argued in Chapter 7, all disclosure by nomination and general election candidates should occur before the election so that voters can consider this information when deciding how to cast their ballots. Pre-election disclosure is currently required only of leadership candidates.

More Proportional Representation

The final proposal advanced here is consideration of reform of the electoral system to include some method of proportional representation. This major reform, the full scope of which is well beyond the borders of this discussion, is considered more fully in John Courtney's volume (2004) in this series. The proposal here is simply that the discussion of whether to adopt proportional representation (PR) should consider its potential both to decrease regional fragmentation and to increase local participation in parties.

A PR system would probably discourage the extreme fragmentation of electoral competition that characterized the last three federal elections of the twentieth century. Under the first-past-the-post system, votes won in areas where a party's candidate is not elected offer no reward. This encourages parties to ignore all those areas of the country where they are not likely to win a plurality of the vote in individual constituencies. The new party system, which has both more parties and at least two major regional parties, has increased the areas of the country in which each party is not competitive. Therefore many Canadians do not receive campaign information from some of the parties. As discussed in Chapter 6, parties are encouraged to be responsive to voters in areas where they might elect members and to ignore others. This leads to regional alienation and makes it difficult for any party to build a national mandate for its proposals.

The second concern is that the system discourages participation from partisans in all of these areas of noncompetitiveness. Liberals in western Canada, Alliance supporters in central and Atlantic Canada, and Conservatives and New Democrats in most parts of the country have no incentive to involve themselves in their party's electoral efforts. The local nomination contests are essentially meaningless as they will not lead to the selection of a member of Parliament, and campaign efforts that might increase the local vote from 15 to 20 percent are equally inconsequential. A system incorporating some measure of PR would reward parties for these incremental increases in voter support and would encourage grassroots participation in all areas of the country.

Parties and Canadian Democracy

As the central players in Canadian democracy, parties carry a heavy burden. If we are to revitalize our politics, encourage more Canadians to participate, and increase voter confidence in our democratic practices, then parties must be at the forefront of any reforms. The discussion in this volume has attempted to highlight the challenges facing the parties and to present a few suggestions as to how they may better respond to voters' needs.

In many respects Canada's political parties are more participatory, inclusive, and responsive than they have ever been. A century ago, women and Aboriginal Canadians did not have the vote, there were no extraparliamentary party members, there was no intraparty policy development, and leaders were chosen by small groups of men in the parliamentary caucuses. By comparison, participation in today's parties is much more inclusive and consequential. Nonetheless, Canadians are not satisfied to have parties that are more democratic than they were in the past, or that may be more democratic than parties in other countries. Rather, they want parties that measure up to their democratic expectations at the outset of the twenty-first century. Much work remains to be done in order for parties to meet this high standard.

POSTSCRIPT

Writing about Canada's political parties is a tricky proposition as they continue to adapt to the electoral earthquake of 1993. In the short period between the writing and the publication of this book the Progressive Conservative and Canadian Alliance parties entered into a formal merger, forming the new Conservative Party of Canada. While it is too soon to be able to say anything definitive about the new party, a few preliminary observations, relevant to the subjects covered in this volume, are appropriate.

One of the most striking things about the new party is that it was formed, chose a leader, and began preparing to wage an election campaign before any meaningful discussion on public policy had been held. The merger agreement between the old parties is silent on questions of policy beyond a list of "founding principles" that for the most part are general motherhood statements acceptable to all. The early commitment of the Reform party to a grassroots-driven policy as the cornerstone of party democracy, as discussed in Chapter 3, seems lost in this new entity, which was essentially created in private talks between party elites and then rubber stamped by party members.

The party has adopted a leadership selection method that is a compromise between those most recently used by the Canadian Alliance and Progressive Conservative parties. Reflecting the Alliance principle of member equality, the choice of Stephen Harper was made through a direct vote of the membership without a delegated convention. Reflecting the Progressive Conservative view of regional equity, the votes were weighed by region, providing each riding with 100 votes. Essentially, this is the method used when Joe Clark was selected as the Tory party leader in 1998. The leadership contest itself was marked by charges of vote buying, membership stacking, and extravagant campaign spending. Fears of voting fraud were expressed by some of the candidates' supporters as the rules allowed for bundled votes to be cast by campaign operatives via fax machines. Nothing in this contest weakens the argument for greater regulation of party leadership selection by Elections Canada.

As the new party prepares for a federal election, we see conflicting signs regarding the local autonomy in candidate nomination that marked Alliance contests. Alliance incumbents seeking renomination as Conservative candidates – including former party leader Stockwell Day and BC MP Val Meredith, who was defeated in her bid – have faced serious challenges. At the same time, the new party's central office has denied former Saskatchewan premier Grant Devine permission to compete for a nomination. The conflicting ethos on party democracy between the two parties remains to be worked out.

The merger of two parties with different regional bases may serve to diminish somewhat the regionalization of electoral competition discussed in Chapter 6, but this is far from certain. The new party begins with the Alliance's western support base. It is unclear whether Tory support in Atlantic Canada will move to the new party. Two high-profile Tory MPs, Scott Brison from Nova Scotia and John Herron from New Brunswick, have refused to join the new party and have instead indicated a desire to run for the Liberals in the next election. The merger may increase the new party's support in Ontario, but the two parties combined are far behind the Liberals and Bloc Québécois in Quebec. Truly national electoral competition may remain elusive for some time.

Discussion Questions

Chapter 1: Auditing Canada's Political Parties

1 What are the principal functions political parties serve in Canadian democracy?

2 Considering that municipal politics in many Canadian cities does not involve political parties, can you imagine a form of Canadian federal politics without parties, or are they essential features of our democracy?

3 Are the benchmarks of participation, inclusiveness, and responsiveness appropriate to an examination of the status of Canadian parties at the outset of the twenty-first century?

Chapter 2: Political Parties As Membership Organizations

1 Why do you think so few young Canadians belong to political parties?

2 What problems does a lack of representativeness in their memberships pose for Canada's parties?

3 What can parties do to attract and retain more members?

Chapter 3: Policy Study and Development

1 Should the parliamentary parties be bound by the policy positions taken by their activist members?

2 Why do Canadians, by a three-to-one margin, believe interest group participation to be a more effective way of influencing public policy than membership in a political party?

3 Can you identify each of the principal federal parties with particular policy positions? If so, are these positions consistent over time?

4 Should the parties receive annual public grants for the purpose of establishing and maintaining policy foundations?

Chapter 4: Candidate Selection

1 Why do only a small percentage of voters participate in nomination contests? Would more voters participate if participation was made easier?

2 Why do so few women enter party nomination contests? Should parties take concrete steps to increase the number of female and minority candidates?

3 From a democratic perspective, is the recruitment of large numbers of noncitizens in some nomination contests good or bad?

4 Should candidate selection be conducted like general election voting, with all voters eligible to participate? What effect would this have on parties as membership organizations?

Chapter 5: Selection of Party Leaders

1 Which of the various methods of leadership selection described in this chapter do you think is the best one? Are different methods better suited to different parties?
2 Should voting in leadership contests be restricted to a party's long-term members, or should all interested Canadians be able to participate? Does it make a difference if the newly chosen leader will immediately become prime minister or premier?
3 Should parties be permitted to charge a fee for voting in a leadership contest?
4 Who should have the authority to remove party leaders?

Chapter 6: Parties and Election Campaigning

1 How has the rise of the Canadian Alliance and the Bloc Québécois affected election campaigning?
2 Are political parties overly dependent on political professionals such as pollsters and advertising specialists? Does this affect the quality of political leadership? Is it related to declining voter turnout?
3 How important are local effects, such as candidates, constituency association vitality, and local issues, to outcomes in constituency-level election results? Do the central parties underestimate these effects?
4 How would the parties' approach to campaigning change if our electoral system included some form of proportional representation?

Chapter 7: Money and Politics

1 Should candidates and parties be limited in the amounts they can spend on campaign activities?
2 Should corporations and trade labour unions be permitted to contribute to parties' and candidates' election coffers?
3 Should public funding be available to support candidates' and parties' campaign efforts? If so, what is the best form (i.e., how should it be administered) and what is the appropriate amount? Will the 2003 legislative reforms make parties too dependent on the public purse?

4   Should the financing of leadership and nomination campaigns be subject to public regulation?

Chapter 8: Four Proposals for Party Reform

1   What grade (A to F) would you assess Canadian parties for each of participation, inclusiveness, and responsiveness? Justify your choices.

Additional Reading

Chapter 1: Auditing Canada's Political Parties

For the historical development of the Canadian party system see James Bickerton, Alain-G. Gagnon, and Patrick J. Smith's *Ties that bind: Parties and voters in Canada* (1999) and R. Kenneth Carty's essay "Three Canadian party systems: An interpretation of the development of national politics" (2001). The principal characteristics of the new party system are discussed in R. Kenneth Carty, William Cross, and Lisa Young, *Rebuilding Canadian party politics* (2000). A good discussion of early Canadian political culture and of the brokerage roots of the party system can be found in André Siegfried's *The race question in Canada* ([1904] 1966). John Meisel provides an overview of the particular challenges facing parties in the second half of the twentieth century in "Decline of party in Canada" (1991). For a comprehensive evaluation of Canadian parties at the end of the twentieth century and a useful discussion of some reform proposals, see the *Report* of the Royal Commission on Electoral Reform and Party Financing (1991) and the accompanying research volumes. A good overview of voter disaffection in many Western democracies is found in Pharr and Putnam's collection, *Disaffected democracies: What's troubling the trilateral countries?* (2000).

Chapter 2: Political Parties As Membership Organizations

A comprehensive discussion of the activities and organization of local party associations is found in R. Kenneth Carty's *Canadian political parties in the constituencies* (1991). Further consideration of issues relating to Canadian party membership, drawing upon the same data used in this chapter, can be found in Lisa Young and my articles "Incentives to membership in Canadian political parties" (2002a) and "The rise of plebiscitary democracy in Canadian political parties" (2002b). Patrick Seyd and Paul Whiteley pioneered the study of party members with their excellent books on the United Kingdom. Interested readers should see their *Labour's grass roots: The politics of party membership* (1992) and *True blues: The politics of Conservative Party membership* (Whiteley, Seyd, and Jeremy Richardson 1994). Michael Gallagher and Michael Marsh have recently published an equally interesting study of members of the Irish Fine Gael party, *Days of blue loyalty: The politics of membership of the Fine Gael Party* (2002). For an excellent comparative overview of the membership crises in many Western democracies, see Susan Scarrow's "Parties without members?" (2000).

Chapter 3: Policy Study and Development

For an overview of the historical efforts at increasing party members' role in policy making, see Carty, Cross, and Young 2000, ch. 6. Stephen Clarkson's essay "Democracy in the Liberal Party: The experiment with citizen participation under Pierre Trudeau" (1979) provides an excellent account of the early attempts to increase the role of party members in policy setting during the Trudeau governments. Clarkson's analysis highlights the ongoing tension between governments and extraparliamentary parties in policy making. In *Absent mandate: Canadian electoral politics in an era of restructuring* (1996), Harold Clarke et al. highlight how the brokerage parties avoid taking stances on issues and remain ideologically flexible in hopes of attracting a broad coalition of election supporters. Gerry Baier and Herman Bakvis examine the relationship between political parties and think-tanks in their article "Think tanks and political parties: Competitors or collaborators?" (2001).

Chapter 4: Candidate Selection

A detailed overview of the candidate nomination process is found in R. Kenneth Carty and Lynda Erickson's "Candidate nomination in Canada's national political parties" (1991). An interesting earlier article that reviews the nomination processes in the 1979 and 1980 federal elections is Robert Williams' "Candidate selection" (1981). My article "Grassroots participation in candidate nominations" (2002a) focuses on the tensions between local authority and increasing central party involvement in the nomination process. The challenges facing women candidates are well presented by Lynda Erickson in "Women and candidacies for the House of Commons" (1991).

Chapter 5: Selection of Party Leaders

For an excellent discussion of both the history and the current challenges surrounding leadership selection in Canada, see John Courtney's *Do conventions matter? Choosing national party leaders in Canada* (1995). This book also includes an interesting chapter on the removal of leaders that includes comparative material. George Perlin's *Party democracy in Canada: The politics of national party conventions* (1988) includes useful information regarding the large national conventions of the 1970s and 1980s. My article "Direct election of provincial party leaders in Canada, 1985-95: The end of the leadership convention?" (1996a) surveys the various methods of direct election used by provincial parties and the issues considered by them when deciding whether to abandon the delegate convention. R. Kenneth Carty, Lynda Erickson, and Donald Blake's collection *Leaders and parties in Canadian politics: Experiences of the provinces* (1992) includes chapters analyzing different selection methods in different provincial parties across the country. This collection presents portraits of the different political cultures found in the regions and their impact on leadership selection. Keith Archer and Alan Whitehorn's *Political activists: The NDP in convention* (1997) provides an insightful overview of leadership politics in the NDP.

Chapter 6: Parties and Election Campaigning

An excellent overview of the parties' campaign strategies in the 2000 federal election is found in Jon H. Pammett and Christopher Dornan's collection *The Canadian general election of 2000* (2001). Similarly, André Blais et al. discuss the dynamics of the 2000 campaign in *Anatomy of a Liberal victory: Making sense of the vote in the 2000 election* (2002). Anthony Sayers' book *Candidates and constituency campaigns in Canadian elections* (1998) includes an interesting portrait of riding-level dynamics during a national campaign and identifies different types of local campaigns. Reginald Whitaker's essay "Virtual political parties and the decline of democracy" (2001) considers the effects of new communications technology on election campaigning. R. Kenneth Carty's book *Canadian political parties in the constituencies* (1991) provides a comprehensive examination of the activities of local party associations both in and out of election campaigns.

Chapter 7: Money and Politics

A good discussion of the period surrounding the adoption of the Canada Elections Act is found in Khayyam Paltiel's essay "Canadian election expenses legislation, 1963-1985: A critical appraisal or was the effort worth it?" (1987). F. Leslie Seidle's collection *Provincial party and election finance in Canada* (1991) provides a useful overview of the different regulatory approaches taken at the provincial level. Carty, Cross, and Young's *Rebuilding Canadian party politics* (2000) includes a chapter examining questions of party financing in light of the new party system. Filip Palda's book *Election finance regulation in Canada* (1991) provides an interesting critique of the Canadian approach to regulating party and candidate financing.

Works Cited

Adamson, Agar, and Bruce Beaton. 1994. Pushing the right buttons: Nova Scotia Liberals and tele-democracy. In *Roasting chestnuts: The mythology of Maritime political culture,* ed. Ian Stewart, 135-54. Vancouver: UBC Press.

Archer, Keith, and Alan Whitehorn. 1997. *Political activists: The NDP in convention.* Toronto: Oxford University Press.

Baier, Gerald, and Herman Bakvis. 2001. Think tanks and political parties: Competitors or collaborators? *Isuma: Canadian Journal of Policy Research* 2(1): 107-13.

Bashevkin, Sylvia. 1993. *Toeing the lines: Women and party politics in English Canada.* 2d ed. Toronto: Oxford University Press.

Bickerton, James, Alain-G. Gagnon, and Patrick J. Smith. 1999. *Ties that bind: Parties and voters in Canada.* Toronto: Oxford University Press.

Blais, André, and Elisabeth Gidengil. 1991. *Making representative democracy work: The views of Canadians.* Toronto: Dundurn Press.

Blais, André, Elisabeth Gidengil, Richard Nadeau, and Neil Nevitte. 2002. *Anatomy of a Liberal victory: Making sense of the vote in the 2000 election.* Peterborough, ON: Broadview Press.

Blake, Donald E., and R. Kenneth Carty. 1994. Televoting for the leader of the British Columbia Liberal Party: The leadership contest of 1993. Paper presented at the meetings of the Canadian Political Science Association. Calgary. June.

Brodie, Janine, and Jane Jenson. 1991. Piercing the smokescreen: Brokerage parties and class politics. In *Canadian parties in transition: Discourse, organization and representation*, ed. Alain Gagnon and A. Brian Tanguay, 52-72. Scarborough, ON: Nelson.

Cameron, David R., and Graham White. 2001. *Cycling into Saigon: The conservative transition in Ontario.* Vancouver: UBC Press.

Carty, R. Kenneth. 1991. *Canadian political parties in the constituencies.* Toronto: Dundurn Press.

—. 2001. Three Canadian party systems: An interpretation of the development of national politics. In *Party politics in Canada,* ed. Hugh G. Thorburn, 16-32. 8th ed. Scarborough, ON: Prentice-Hall.

—. 2002. The politics of Tecumseh Corner. *Canadian Journal of Political Science* 35(4): 723-45.

Carty, R. Kenneth, William Cross, and Lisa Young. 2000. *Rebuilding Canadian party politics.* Vancouver: UBC Press.

Carty, R. Kenneth, and Munroe Eagles. Forthcoming. *Politics is local: Parties and elections in Canada.* Toronto: Oxford University Press.

Carty, R. Kenneth, and Lynda Erickson. 1991. Candidate nomination in Canada's national political parties. In *Canadian political parties: Leaders, candidates and organization,* ed. Herman Bakvis, 97-190. Toronto: Dundurn Press.

Carty, R. Kenneth, Lynda Erickson, and Donald Blake, eds. 1992. *Leaders and parties in Canadian politics: Experiences of the provinces.* Toronto: Harcourt Brace Jovanovich Canada.

Chandler, William, and Allen Siaroff. 1991. Parties and party government in advanced democracies. In *Canadian political parties: Leaders, candidates and organization,* ed. Herman Bakvis, 191-264. Toronto: Dundurn Press.

Clarke, Harold D., Jane Jenson, Lawrence LeDuc, and Jon H. Pammett. 1996. *Absent mandate: Canadian electoral politics in an era of restructuring.* 3d ed. Toronto: Gage Publishing.

Clarkson, Stephen. 1979. Democracy in the Liberal Party: The experiment with citizen participation under Pierre Trudeau. In *Party Politics in Canada,* ed. Hugh G. Thorburn. 4th ed. Scarborough, ON: Prentice-Hall.

—. 2001. The Liberal threepeat: The multi-system party in the multi-party system. In *The Canadian general election of 2000,* ed. Jon H. Pammett and Christopher Dornan, 13-58. Toronto: Dundurn Press.

Courtney, John. 1973. *The selection of national party leaders in Canada.* Toronto: Macmillan.

—. 1995. *Do conventions matter? Choosing national party leaders in Canada.* Montreal: McGill-Queen's University Press.

—. 2004. *Elections.* Canadian Democratic Audit. Vancouver: UBC Press.

Cross, William. 1992. Financing federal party leadership campaigns. MA thesis, University of Western Ontario, London.

—. 1996a. Direct election of provincial party leaders in Canada, 1985-95: The end of the leadership convention? *Canadian Journal of Political Science* 29(2): 295-315.

—. 1996b. Grassroots participation in Canadian political parties: An examination of leadership selection, candidate nomination, policy development and election campaigning. PhD diss., University of Western Ontario, London.

—. 1998. The conflict between participatory and accommodative politics: The case for stronger parties. *International Journal of Canadian Studies* 17 (Spring): 37-55.

—. 2002a. Grassroots participation in candidate nominations. In *Citizen politics: Research and theory in Canadian political behaviour,* ed. Joanna Everitt and Brenda O'Neill, 373-85. Toronto: Oxford University Press.

—. 2002b. The increased importance of region in Canadian political campaigns. In *Regionalism and party politics in Canada*, ed. Lisa Young and Keith Archer, 116-28. Toronto: Oxford University Press.

—. 2002c. Leadership selection in New Brunswick: Balancing language represen-tation and populist impulses. In *Political parties, representation, and electoral democracy in Canada*, ed. William Cross, 37-54. Toronto: Oxford University Press.

Cross, William, and Ian Stewart. 2002. Ethnicity and accommodation in the New Brunswick party system. *Journal of Canadian Studies* 36(4): 32-58.

Cross, William, and Lisa Young. 2002. Policy attitudes of party members in Canada: Evidence of ideological politics. *Canadian Journal of Political Science* 35(4): 859-80.

Dalton, Russell J., and Martin P. Wattenberg. 2000. *Parties without partisans: Political change in advanced industrial democracies.* Oxford: Oxford University Press.

Dawson, R. MacGregor. 1947. *The government of Canada.* London: Oxford Univer-sity Press.

Docherty, David. 2004. *Legislatures.* Canadian Democratic Audit. Vancouver and Toronto: UBC Press.

Elections Canada. 2000. Candidates' 2000 election returns. <www.elections.ca> (28 January 2004).

Ellis, Faron. 2001. The more things change ... The Alliance campaign. In *The Cana-dian general election of 2000*, ed. Jon H. Pammett and Christopher Dornan, 59-90. Toronto: Dundurn Press.

Erickson, Lynda. 1991. Women and candidacies for the House of Commons. In *Women in Canadian politics: Towards equity in representation*, ed. Kathy Megyery, 101-26. Toronto: Dundurn Press.

—. 1993. Making her way in: Women, parties and candidacies in Canada. In *Gender and party politics*, ed. Joni Lovenduski and Pippa Norris, 60-85. London: Sage.

Gallagher, Michael, and Michael Marsh. 2002. *Days of blue loyalty: The politics of membership of the Fine Gael Party.* Dublin: PSAI Press.

Gidengil, Elisabeth, and Joanna Everitt. 2002. Damned if you do, damned if you don't: Television news coverage of female party leaders in the 1993 federal election. In *Political parties, representation, and electoral democracy in Canada*, ed. William Cross, 223-37. Toronto: Oxford University Press.

Harper, Tim. 2000. Abortion foes seek voice in Alliance. *Toronto Star,* 3 September, A3.

Harrington, Carol. 2000. Voting for citizens only, Alliance MP urges. *Toronto Star,* 2 October, A20.

Howe, Paul, and David Northrup. 2000. *Strengthening Canadian democracy: The views of Canadians*. Policy Matters series vol. 1, no 5. Ottawa: Institute for Research on Public Policy.

Johnson, David. 1991. The Ontario party and campaign finance system: initiative and challenge. In *Provincial party and election finance in Canada*, ed. F. Leslie Seidle. Toronto: Dundurn Press.

Johnston, Richard, André Blais, Henry Brady, and Jean Crete. 1992. *Letting the people decide: Dynamics of a Canadian election*. Montreal: McGill-Queen's University Press.

King, Anthony. 1969. Political parties in Western democracies. *Polity* 2 (Winter): 111-41.

Leadership rules spark revolt. 1989. *Toronto Star,* 2 September, A9.

Lee, Robert Mason. 1989. *One hundred monkeys: The triumph of popular wisdom in Canadian politics*. Toronto: Macfarlane, Walter and Ross.

Liberal Party of Canada. 1990. Untitled release. 7 November.

MacEwan, Paul. 1993. Reforming the leadership convention process: A round table discussion. *Canadian Parliamentary Review* 16(3): 5-11.

Marzolini, Michael. 2001. The politics of values: Designing the 2000 Liberal campaign. In *The Canadian General Election of 2000,* ed. Jon Pammett and Christopher Dornan, 263-76. Toronto: Dundurn Press.

Massicotte, Louis. 1991. Party financing in Quebec. In *Provincial party and election finance in Canada*, ed. F. Leslie Seidle, 3-28. Toronto: Dundurn Press.

—. 2001. Financing parties at the grass-root level: The Quebec experience. Paper presented at meetings of The Money in Politics International Group, Florence, Italy, November.

Meisel, John. 1991. Decline of party in Canada. In *Party politics in Canada,* ed. Hugh G. Thorburn, 178-201. 6th ed. Scarborough, ON: Prentice-Hall.

Nevitte, Neil. 1996. *The decline of deference: Canadian value change in cross-national perspective*. Peterborough, ON: Broadview Press.

New Democratic Party. 1997. Nomination and affirmative action policy. Policy document.

Noel, S.J.R. 1971. *Politics in Newfoundland*. Toronto: University of Toronto Press.

Palda, Filip. 1991. *Election finance regulation in Canada*. Vancouver: Fraser Institute.

Paltiel, Khayyam. 1987. Canadian election expenses legislation, 1963-1985: A critical appraisal or was the effort worth it? In *Contemporary Canadian politics*, ed. Robert J. Jackson, 228-47. Scarborough, ON: Prentice-Hall.

Pammett, Jon H., and Christopher Dornan, eds. 2001. *The Canadian general election of 2000*. Toronto: Dundurn Press.

Perlin, George. 1991a. Attitudes of Liberal convention delegates towards proposals for reform of the process of leadership selection. In *Canadian political parties: Leaders, candidates and organizations*, ed. Herman Bakvis, 57-96. Toronto: Dundurn Press.

—. 1991b. Leadership selection in the Progressive Conservative and Liberal Parties: Assessing the need for reform. In *Party politics in Canada,* ed. Hugh G. Thorburn, 202-20. 6th ed. Scarborough, ON: Prentice-Hall.

—, ed. 1988. *Party democracy in Canada: The politics of national party conventions.* Scarborough, ON: Prentice-Hall Canada.

Pharr, Susan J., and Robert D. Putnam, eds. 2000. *Disaffected democracies: What's troubling the trilateral countries?* Princeton, NJ: Princeton University Press.

Progressive Conservative Party of Canada. 1994. Background paper on restructuring. Policy document.

Royal Commission on Electoral Reform and Party Financing. 1991. *Report.* 2 vols. Ottawa: Ministry of Supply and Services.

Sabato, Larry. 1981. *The rise of political consultants.* New York: Basic Books.

Savoie, Donald. 1999. *Governing from the centre: The concentration of power in Canadian politics.* Toronto: University of Toronto Press.

Sayers, Anthony. 1998. *Candidates and constituency campaigns in Canadian elections.* Vancouver: UBC Press.

Scarrow, Harold A. 1964. Nomination and local party organization in Canada: A case study. *Western Political Quarterly* 17: 55-62.

Scarrow, Susan. 2000. Parties without members? Party organization in a changing electoral environment. In *Disaffected democracies: What's troubling the trilateral countries?* ed. Susan J. Pharr and Robert D. Putnam, 129-56. Princeton, NJ: Princeton University Press.

Schattschneider. 1942. Party government. New York: Rinehart.

Seidle, F. Leslie, ed. 1991. *Provincial party and election finance in Canada.* Toronto: Dundurn Press.

Seyd, Patrick, and Paul Whiteley. 1992. *Labour's grass roots: The politics of party membership.* Oxford: Clarendon.

—. 2002. *New Labour's grass roots.* Basingstoke, UK: Palgrave.

Siegfried, André. [1904] 1966. *The race question in Canada.* Rev. ed., edited by Frank Underhill. Toronto: McClelland and Stewart.

Simpson, Jeffrey. 2001. *The friendly dictatorship.* Toronto: McClelland and Stewart.

Smith, Sarah. Just like home: Tim Hortons. December 17-24, 01. *Marketing Magazine* 106(50): 27.

Stewart, David K. 1997. The changing electorate: An examination of participants in the 1992 Alberta Conservative leadership election. *Canadian Journal of Political Science* 30(1): 107-28.

Stewart, David K., and R. Kenneth Carty. 2002. Leadership politics as party building: The Conservatives in 1998. In *Political parties, representation, and electoral democracy in Canada*, ed. William Cross, 55-67. Toronto: Oxford University Press.

Thompson, Elizabeth. 1990. The sky's the limit: Liberal candidates bending rules on spending. *Montreal Gazette,* 31 March, B6.

Thunert, Martin. 2003. Conservative think tanks in the United States and Canada. In *Conservative parties and right-wing politics in North America: Reaping the benefits of an ideological victory?* ed. Rainer-Olaf Schultze, Roland Sturm, and Dagmar Eberle, 229-54. Opladen, Germany: Leske and Budrich.

Toulin, Alan. 1998. Honesty made easy. *Financial Post,* v. 91, 23-5 May, 10.

Wearing, Joseph. 1981. *The L-shaped party: The Liberal Party of Canada 1958-1980.* Toronto: McGraw-Hill Ryerson.

Whitaker, Reginald. 1977. *The government party: Organizing and financing the Liberal Party of Canada, 1930-1958.* Toronto: University of Toronto Press.

—. 2001. Virtual political parties and the decline of democracy. *Policy Options* (June): 16-22.

White, Graham. 2005. *Cabinets and First Ministers.* Canadian Democratic Audit. Vancouver and Toronto: UBC Press.

Whitehorn, Alan. 2001. The 2000 NDP campaign: Social democracy at the crossroads. In *The Canadian general election of 2000*, ed. Jon H. Pammett and Christopher Dornan, 113-38. Toronto: Dundurn Press.

Whiteley, Paul, and Patrick Seyd. 2003. Party election campaigning in Britain: The Labour Party. *Party Politics* 9(5): 637-52.

Whiteley, Paul, Patrick Seyd, and Jeremy Richardson. 1994. *True blues: The politics of Conservative Party membership.* Oxford: Clarendon.

Williams, Robert. 1981. Candidate selection. In *Canada at the polls, 1979 and 1980: A study of the general elections,* ed. Howard R. Penniman, 86-120. Washington: American Enterprise Institute for Research in Public Policy.

Winsor, Hugh. 1992. Liberals clean up nomination process: Recruitment of instant members and ethnic minority groups to end. *Globe and Mail,* 21 February, A1.

Woolstencroft, Peter. 2001. Some battles won, war lost: The campaign of the Progressive Conservative Party. In *The Canadian general election of 2000,* ed. Jon H. Pammett and Christopher Dornan, 91-112. Toronto: Dundurn Press.

Young, Lisa. 1998. Party, state and political competition in Canada. *Canadian Journal of Political Science* 31(2): 339-58.

—. 2000. *Feminists and party politics.* Vancouver: UBC Press.

Young, Lisa, and William Cross. 2002a. Incentives to membership in Canadian political parties. *Political Research Quarterly* 55(3): 547-69.

—. 2002b. The rise of plebiscitary democracy in Canadian political parties. *Party Politics* 8(6): 673-99.

Young, Robert. 1991. Effecting change: Do we have the political system to get us where we want to go? In *Canada at risk? Canadian public policy in the 1990s,* ed. G. Bruce Doern and Bryne B. Purchase, 59-80. Toronto: CD Howe Institute.

Index

Ablonczy, Diane, 23
Aboriginal peoples, at leadership conventions, 81
Aboriginal People's Commission, 22
advertising, in election campaigns, 109, 114, 124-5, 130-1, 133, 134
affirmative action: in candidate selection, 53; in NDP, 70-1
Alberta: Alliance in, 94, 128, 129; Calgary Northeast riding, 65; Conservatives in, 127, 160 (*see also* Progressive Conservative [PC] Party [AB]); Liberal Party in, 17, 127; neoconservatism in, 17
Alliance. *See* Canadian Alliance
Anders, Rob, 23, 66
Asian Canadian community, 52
Atlantic Canada: Alliance in, 160, 183; Conservatives in, 16, 17, 94, 127, 128, 130; Liberals in, 128, 133-4; NDP in, 94, 127, 160; parties in, 24. *See also* names of provinces
Augustine, Jean, 60
Australia: leadership selection in, 91; party membership in, 19
Axworthy, Lloyd, 82-3, 164, 165

Beatty, Perrin, 35, 82-3, 165
Blaikie, Bill, 42
Blakeney, Alan, 42
Bloc Québécois, 7, 157; in 1993 election, 18; in 2000 election, 126-7; corporate contributions to, 146, 147t; direct elections for leaders, 84; election campaigns, 135, 138; ethnic minority candidates, 68; as federal party, 16; francophones in, 23-4; geographical concentration, 23-4; on leaders' influence, 39; leadership selection, 84, 106; local campaigns and, 109; member satisfaction with, 28, 29; members, and policy development, 25, 38; participation rates, 27, 28; policy conventions, 38; public financing for, 157, 158, 159; in Quebec, 128; riding-based voting by, 86; union contributions to, 146, 147t
Britain. *See* United Kingdom
British Columbia: Alliance in, 16, 94, 128, 129; Conservatives in,

159-60; Liberals in, 16, 17, 93, 127, 129; NDP of, 16, 160; popular vs winning vote, 125
Broadview-Greenwood (Toronto) riding, 115
brokerage parties, 7, 44, 178; ideological parties vs, 9, 25, 38; interest groups and, 9; policies, and membership, 25; policy institutes and, 44
brokerage politics, 9, 38, 46, 172, 177; and policy innovation, 45

cabinet, policy making by, 34, 45
Caledon Institution of Social Policy, 42
Calvert, Lorne, 99
campaign finance: 2003 reform legislation, 41, 73, 143, 153-4, 166-7, 167, 180; abuses, 142; accessibility and, 143, 144, 154, 155, 166, 167; and allies of candidates/parties, 145; banks and, 148, 149-50t; and communication with voters, 151, 180; competitiveness and, 144, 156; corporate contributions (*see* corporate contributions); definition of election expenses, 161; disclosure of (*see* disclosure); equity and, 143, 154, 155, 166; free-market approach, 143-4; and inclusiveness, 143, 144, 167; influence of, 142, 163; in Manitoba, 150; participation and, 143, 144, 167; probity, 143, 166; in Quebec, 150, 151; reform, 8, 172, 180-2; regulation, 142-4; and responsiveness, 142, 167; and special interests, 144, 146, 167, 180; spending limits (*see* spending limits); and television, 151, 161; trade union contributions (*see* trade union contributions); transparency, 143, 153, 166
Campaign Life Coalition, 64
Campbell, Kim, 35-6, 82, 83, 99, 164, 181
Canada Election Study (2000), 148
Canada Elections Act, 54, 143, 145, 155; 2003 reform legislation, 41, 143, 167, 176, 180
Canadian Alliance, 7-8; activities of members, 26, 27; in Alberta, 94, 128, 129; in Atlantic Canada, 160, 183; in British

Columbia, 16, 94, 128, 129; campaign advertising, 131; campaigns, 127-8, 130, 133, 135, 138; candidates, 63, 64, 68, 71-2, 177; in central Canada, 183; and citizenship requirements, 66; on constituent groups, 23, 71; constitution, 61; corporate contributions to, 146, 147t; in eastern Canada, 94; as federal party, 16; francophones in, 23; geographical concentration, 24; grassroots supporters in, 63; individuals vs groups in, 23; and interest groups on right, 42; leadership contests, 89-90, 94; leadership removal, 104; leadership selection, 106; mail-in voting by, 85; members, and policy, 25, 38; membership characteristics, 20-1, 23, 28, 29; in Ontario, 126, 128, 133, 160; participation rates, 26, 27, 28; policy conventions, 38; policy positions of candidates, 63; and politics of special interests, 23; public financing for, 157, 158, 159; in Quebec, recruitment of Sikh members, 65; regional representation and, 94; renomination of incumbents in, 61; riding-based voting, 86; in Saskatchewan, 129; spending by, 72, 162, 164; telephone voting by, 85; United Alternative project, 89; visible minorities in, 23, 68; in western Canada, 73, 126; women in, 20, 23, 68; youth in, 23. *See also* Conservative Party of Canada; Reform Party
Canadian Broadcasting Corporation (CBC), 114; privatization of, 35
Canadian Centre for Policy Alternatives, 42
Canadian Democratic Audit project, 6
Canadian Taxpayers Federation (CTF), 42
candidate nomination, 49; attendance at meetings, 56, 59, 62; central party control, 176-7; choice of locations, 57-8, 173; citizenship requirements for

caucus   Tories
federalism   laissez-faire
incumbent
centralized
balkanization
Disclosure